LANDS' END® BUSINESS ATTIRE FOR MEN

LANDS' END
BUSINESS ATTIRE FOR
MEN
MASTERING THE NEW ABCs
OF WHAT TO WEAR TO WORK

LANDS' END

TEXT BY TODD LYON

CLARKSON POTTER/ PUBLISHERS
NEW YORK

A Stonesong Press Book
Published by Clarkson Potter/Publishers, New York, New York
Member of the Crown Publishing Group, a division of Random House, Inc.
www.crownpublishing.com

CLARKSON N. POTTER is a trademark and POTTER and colophon are registered trademarks of Random House, Inc.

Printed in Singapore

Book design by Blue Cup Creative, Inc./Wayne Wolf

Illustrations by Rachael Phillips

Library of Congress Cataloging-in-Publication Data
Lands' End business attire for men: mastering the new ABCs of what to wear to work /
Lands' End ; text by Todd Lyon.
1. Men's clothing.   I. Lyon, Todd.   II. Lands' End, Inc.
     TT618.L36   2004
     646'.32–dc22   2003058096

ISBN 0-609-61020-1

10   9   8   7   6   5   4   3   2   1

First Edition

To

Ben, Bill, Bob, Brad, Bubs, Bud, Charles, Chris, Collin, Dashiell, David, Duncan, Dylan, Earl, Ernst, Frank, George, Greg, Harry, Hayward, Henri, James, Jamie, Jim, Jody, John, José, Kevin, Mark, Matthew, Michael, Mike, Nick, Paul, Phil, Philip, Ray, Richard, Rick, Seth, Steve, Steven, Taylor, Todd, Tom, Trevor,

and all the other men in my life who manage to look like a million bucks—even, sometimes, when they don't have to.

—T.L.

ACKNOWLEDGMENTS

I thought I knew a thing or two about menswear until I visited Lands' End headquarters in Dodgeville, Wisconsin. There, I studied at the feet of kindly scholars who, collectively, possess an almost encyclopedic knowledge of men's fashions, ranging from necktie patterns to the cut of trench coats. Their passion for detail and dedication to quality is the beating heart of this book. That enlightening trip to Dodgeville never would have happened, however, if it wasn't for my wonderful agent, Colleen Mohyde. She introduced me to Ellen Scordato of Stonesong Press, who initiated and facilitated the project with a sharp eye and a steady hand. Rachael Phillips created the delicious, delicate illustrations, and Katie Workman and Annetta Hanna of Crown Publishers ushered the book into the world. Behind the scenes, my friends, family, and loved ones came through—as they always do—with research, clippings, advice, and feedback. This was indeed a collaborative project, and I thank each and every person who contributed his or her energy and expertise to help make it come true.

—T.L.

CONTENTS

INTRODUCTION: WHAT IS BUSINESS CASUAL?

When the tradition-steeped Yale Club

in Manhattan adopted a business casual dress code in May 2001, it sent a memo to its members outlining the new rules. "Business casual dress consists of professional and tasteful clothing you would wear in your workplace," it read. "If you have any doubt as to whether you are dressed appropriately, you probably are not."

The club's instructions—forceful yet nebulous—raise questions that shoot squarely into the heart of today's business attire dilemma. What, exactly, is professional and tasteful clothing? What magical garb can make you a star at the office, let alone a respected member of a private club, while still being "casual"? In these tumultuous times, who doesn't have doubts about the appropriateness of his attire?

The Yale Club's leap into the modern world had been a long time coming. The seeds of business casual, according to some, were first sown as far back as 1960, when the employees of a prestigious Big Eight accounting firm were no longer required to wear hats to work—though they were required to at least carry them. John F. Kennedy, the first hatless U.S. president, shortly thereafter established the hat-free look for good.

Standard business attire, consisting of three-piece suits, ties, pressed and starched shirts, and the occasional hat, held fast for a number of years after the Kennedy administration—give or take a few lapses into wide ties, peacock-colored shirts, and polyester leisure suits in the '60s and '70s. It wasn't until the 1990s, when high-tech

Casual wear: The 1920s ushered in plus fours, which were quickly ushered out.

CRISIS MANAGEMENT

Q: Rumor has it that my company is going to adopt a business casual policy. One of my fellow workers—who hates looking like a "suit"–is all fired up about finally being able to "express himself." I can't imagine that my conservative bosses would allow much expression of any kind, especially when it comes to clothes. Who's right?

A: You are. Probably.

In virtually all professional environments, certain forms of "self-expression" are frowned upon. Clothes with slogans, logos, oversized designer labels, or any other message-bearing motifs do not belong in the office; like-wise, business casual is not an invitation to become a walking billboard for your favorite team, your favorite band, or your political views. Subversive messages are especially taboo, no matter how passionate your belief.

When conservative offices like yours relax their dress codes, the shift is usually subtle. Maybe you won't have to wear a suit every day, but you'll still need pressed shirts, dress pants, and blazers. And if your friend is thinking about wearing bright orange shirts and Def Leppard ties, he should think again: Flamboyant or eccentric garb doesn't belong in conservative workplaces, even after the office in question has rallied around the business casual flag.

industries launched a small army of dot-com employees into the marketplace, that business casual flourished. In some industries, success was marked not by wearing expensive Italian suits and silk ties, but by donning chinos and loafers. In the opinion of Christine Wright-Isak, a former vice president of Young & Rubicam: "When we receive recognition for actual accomplishment, we are less inclined to use external expressions like clothes to prove it."

In the once-booming "new economy" companies, ingenuity and productivity took precedence over conformity and correctness. Many traditionally dressed businessmen were labeled "suits" and found themselves cut out of the loop. "Individuality has become the thing," said Judy McGrath, president of MTV, in 1995. "The notion of dressing to look like you belong to a company—that doesn't even enter the consciousness anymore. Clothes are more about having a life."

To further advance the march of business casual, a hiring crunch in the late 1990s had recruiters scrambling to find perks that would attract the best and the brightest to their firms. And one of the most attractive benefits, they found, was a relaxed dress code. As eti-

TOP

TEN

CASUAL MISTAKES

FOR MEN

1. Shirts or jackets with slogans, team logos, or prominent brand names*

2. Mistaking "sporting goods" for "sportswear"

3. Pants without belts

4. Inappropriate footwear (athletic shoes, hiking boots, cowboy boots, jackboots, sandals, etc.)

5. Torn, ripped, threadbare, or faded jeans

6. Logoed, sleeveless, or stained T-shirts

7. Clothes that don't fit or flatter

8. Loud or trendy items such as mesh shirts, big jewelry, multiple body piercings, visible tattoos, rock 'n' roll haircuts

9. Tired, worn-out clothes and shoes

10. Caps (the baseball kind)

* *Note:* It's usually acceptable to display small, discreet logos of your alma mater, favorite team, or place of work embroidered above the breast pocket of your shirt.

quette expert Letitia Baldrige noted, "Many senior managers look upon casual dressing as a low-risk morale booster and a perceived employee benefit."

It has taken some time for business casual to become somewhat standardized. At first, the new rules of dress were fraught with confusion and, in some cases, abuse. Back in the '90s, when Mattel, Inc., first decided to make every day casual day, a group of senior executives—including the CEO— came to work in bathrobes, motorcycle jackets, and other inappropriate out- fits, in order to demonstrate how *not* to interpret the company's newly relaxed code of dress.

Stories of casual-gone-wrong have echoed down the corridors of business for years. We know of one retiree who, when paying a call to his investment broker's office, saw a young administrative assistant wearing a T-shirt that read, EAT THE RICH. Another friend remembers the infamous Friday that she kept an appointment with her insurance agent. She arrived to find the normally dig- nified agency overrun with employees clad in denim, fleece, and athletic shoes; when her personal agent came to greet her, he was sporting a sweat- shirt that had I'M SURROUNDED BY IDIOTS emblazoned across the back.

Such stories underscore certain misconceptions that cling to the concept of business casual. To this day, there are great numbers of employees who think that a dressing-down pol- icy means anything goes. Keep in mind that business casual is not synonymous with anarchy. However, the new rules of dressing for success are more complicated than they've ever been. Scott Omelianuk, writing in the *Wall Street Journal*,

Office wear: This outfit would be acceptable from the 1920s to today!

CRISIS MANAGEMENT

Q: After four years spent working in a totally laid-back place, I'm about to take a job in an office with a "business casual" dress code. What's the difference between business casual and plain old casual?

A: "Casual" and "business casual" are entirely different animals. "Casual" is a vast and vague term that's open to interpretation; in most cases, it describes how you dress when you go to a ball game, walk the dog, pick up Chinese food, or catch a blues band at your neighborhood club. Casual is low-key, off-hand, convenient.

Business casual, on the other hand, is a specific, targeted way of dressing. Though the clothes may be less formal and more comfortable than traditional business attire, the rules of business casual are, ironically enough, quite restrictive in terms of what's acceptable and what is not.

To visualize the difference between "casual" and "business casual," imagine a high-school classroom. The students are a motley and colorful bunch, dressed in baggy pants, sneakers, jeans, flannel shirts, athletic garb, knit hats, trendy tees, and the like. Though there may be some sharp dressers in the crowd, the class is, as a group, casual. Now look at the teacher. He's wearing pressed khakis, a sweater vest, an oxford shirt with a button-down collar, and leather shoes. That's business casual. Though his outfit is not stiff or stuffy, it is definitely professional, and it places him in a separate category from the kids. The look underscores his position of authority, yet it's relaxed enough that he doesn't seem fearsome or unapproachable.

And now for the short answer: "Casual" is whatever you feel like wearing. "Business casual" is not.

put his thumb on the buzzer with this statement: "Done right, it's not 'dressing down' at all: It's dressing up in a less traditionally formal way."

Traditional is easy; casual is confusing. The challenge—and it is a challenge, make no mistake—is to identify the parameters of your ideal professional look and create a personal style that fits, in every sense of the word. The purpose of this book is to cut through a jungle of interpretations and establish practical guidelines for all levels of business casual dressing. In the end it will help you to build a working wardrobe that is at once appropriate, flexible, flattering, and fruitful, not to mention right for your particular workplace.

SHIRT
Pinpoint shirt, with French cuffs
and a straight collar, white

SUIT
Year'rounder® suit,
two-button, navy, with
plain-front pants

TIE
Solid rep tie, lime

CUFF LINKS
Soft square cuff
links, silver

BRACES
Fabric braces,
dark navy

SHOES
Perforated cap-toed
oxfords, black

TRADITIONAL BUSINESS ATTIRE

There was a time when men of power wore elaborate garb to show their wealth and importance. Ermine capes, embroidered tunics, velvet pantaloons, gems on every finger—that is how heads of state and captains of commerce dressed for success. Today, the playing field has been leveled, fashion-wise. Instead of wearing golden threads and jeweled buttons, men from all over the world conduct business in simple, conservative suits. Presidents, CEOs, candidates, kings . . . they all understand that the dark suit is a symbol of power and professionalism.

The internationally accepted business suit features a single-breasted jacket and pleated pants. It's made of lightweight wool, in navy blue or charcoal, with or without subtle pinstripes. In its most traditional incarnation, it's paired with a crisp white shirt and a tie with a pattern that's been popular since your grandfather's day. The suit may be worn with a vest (aka "a waistcoat"), suspenders (aka "braces"), or a conservative belt.

Although this is commonly known as a "buttoned-down" look, the shirt has a straight collar that is not, in fact, buttoned down. French cuffs are optional, and thus, so are cuff links. What's nonnegotiable are dark leather shoes (preferably black oxfords) and dark silk socks.

For some men, the traditional business suit is a daily uniform. For others, it is an outfit worn only in high-stakes circumstances. But even if your working situation never requires anything dressier than jeans and sneakers, it's smart to have a suit like this in your closet because it's also standard garb for weddings, funerals, semiformal affairs, and job interviews, should your fortunes take a turn.

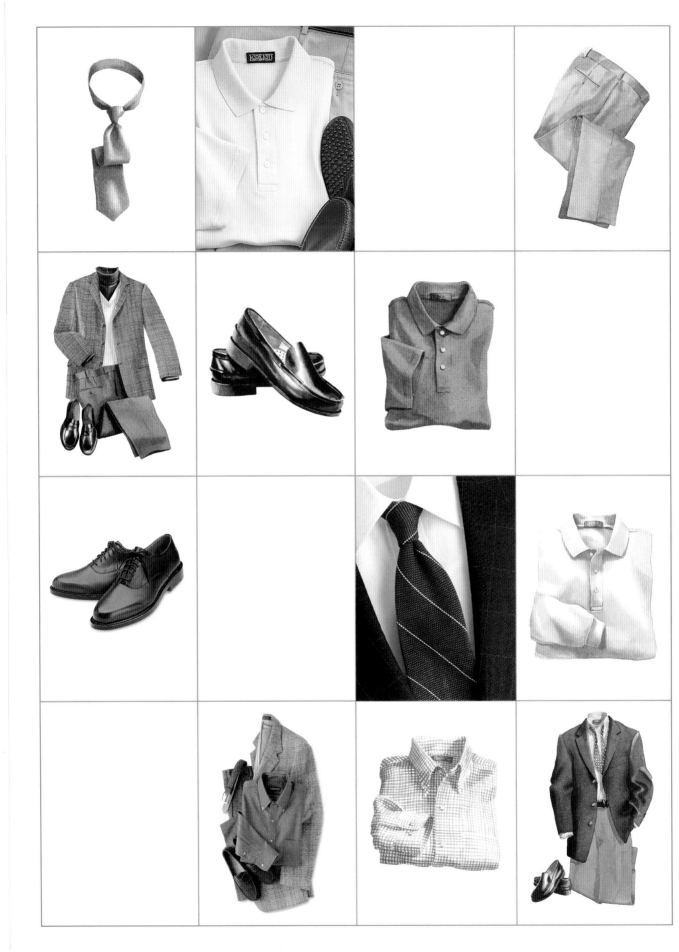

1

DETERMINING YOUR LEVEL OF BUSINESS CASUAL

Business casual rules aren't cast in stone.

Some men might be perfectly turned out in denim shirts and chinos Tuesday through Friday, then snap into a tie and blazer for Monday staff meetings.

That's pretty easy. What's more challenging are positions that call for flexibility, in which a sport coat is on and off again throughout the day. A film director, for instance, might have to crawl around on location all morning, then meet with investors that afternoon. When a wine rep conducts a tasting at a restaurant, he's got to look presentable and somehow dignify the comfortable clothes that have allowed him to haul cases of bottles in and out of his car for hours beforehand.

There are plenty of confusing situations, too. A guy who works in a photo lab doesn't have to worry about how he looks. But when he's promoted to regional manager, and suddenly represents his team as well as his company, jeans and sneakers just won't do. How can he look official and responsible while still remaining casual?

Relax. No matter where you work or what you do, there is a baseline level of business casual that informs your working wardrobe.

Where do you fit in? There are a few ways to find out. First, you should check your company's official dress code, if one exists, which will at least identify items of clothing that you shouldn't wear. Second, look at how your colleagues dress, just to see how they've interpreted the business casual mode. Generally, using your peers as a guide is problematic, but there might be one or two associates who look particularly sharp and whom you may want to emulate.

Of course, these steps won't help much if you're a senior officer or a free agent.

That's where the Business Casual Quiz (opposite) comes in. It can help put you on the right fashion track, no matter if you're a clerk, a consultant, a scientist, or a copywriter.

The
BUSINESS CASUAL
QUIZ

*Is your pencil sharpened? Is your mind clear? Excellent. You're ready
to be tested on your level of business casual.*

INSTRUCTIONS

Look at the four outfits pictured on the following pages.

✶

Imagine that each outfit has magically appeared in your closet
and fits you perfectly.

✶

Using the multiple-choice options, rate the outfits in relation
to your current business needs.

✶

Be aware that there are no "right" or "wrong" answers.

✶

The Business Casual Quiz is based on your honest assessment
of your occupation and working environment.

✶

Finally, turn to "The Results and How to Interpret Them,"
on page 29.

SHIRT
Long-sleeved broad-cloth shirt with straight collar, white

TIE
Silk tie, red dotted with white

SUIT
Wool suit, pinstriped, dark charcoal heather

BELT
Crocodile-embossed belt, black

SHOES
Cap-toed oxfords, black

A | A classic pinstripe suit, complete with white shirt and "power" tie. How would you use it in your business life? *(Check all that apply.)*

☐ I would make it part of my regular office wardrobe. TT AS

☐ I'd wear it to important meetings, presentations, conferences, and the like. AS BB

☐ It's too formal for my day-to-day job. BB CC

☐ It doesn't jibe with my occupation; I probably wouldn't wear it even for job interviews or special meetings. CC

SHIRT
Long-sleeved cotton
shirt, blue striped

TIE
Silk tie with a small floral
pattern, khaki tones

JACKET
Three-button jacket,
hopsack, navy

BELT
Leather belt,
dark brown

SHOES
Plain-vamp loafers,
dark brown

PANTS
Plain-front pants, khaki

B A navy blazer, a subtly striped shirt, khaki-colored pants, and a coordinating tie, paired with loafers and a brown belt. How would you put this ensemble to work?
(Check all that apply.)

☐ I'd wear it only on designated casual days. TT

☐ I'd put it on for significant events at the office. AS BB CC

☐ It would become part of my regular working wardrobe. AS BB

☐ I'd probably save it for my private life; it's too dressed-up for my workplace. CC

SCORING

Look at each answer that you checked off. To the right of each answer is one or more coded initials: TT, AS, BB, CC. Tally up these initials and mark the totals below.

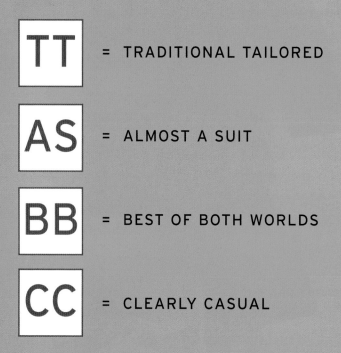

TT = TRADITIONAL TAILORED

AS = ALMOST A SUIT

BB = BEST OF BOTH WORLDS

CC = CLEARLY CASUAL

The category in which you scored the most points indicates your general level of business casual. Knowing your type will help steer you toward creating a wardrobe that's right for you, your job, and your place of business.

THE RESULTS AND HOW TO INTERPRET THEM

DEFINING THE ARCHETYPES

If you scored highest in the Traditional Tailored (TT) category, you probably work in a conservative office and have adopted a profession in which dignity, reliability, and old-fashioned values are signaled via sober suits and ties. So how can business casual apply to you? Because it is buttoned-up professionals like yourself who are often most baffled when their offices suddenly institute casual days.

If you scored highest in the Almost a Suit (AS) category, your place of business is probably professional in spirit, but not steeped in tradition. Blazers and trousers replace suits, ties are optional, and polished loafers can stand in for wing-tip oxfords.

If you scored highest in the Best of Both Worlds (BB) category, you likely have a number of working roles that call for a laid-back look on some days and a businesslike ensemble on other days. BB is the most flexible category of dress, and outfits may include everything from chinos and a polo shirt to a sport coat, dress trousers, and a tie.

If you scored highest in the Clearly Casual (CC) category, chances are your job requires little or no public contact. CC types rarely have a need for neckties or blazers, but they do need to look neat, coordinated, and appropriate.

YOU MIGHT BE A "TT" TYPE IF YOU

* work in banking, law, politics, finance, or insurance
* have a high-level title (CEO, CFO, COO, chairman of the board, anchorman, diplomat, elected official, president, founder, owner, partner, director, judge, attorney, publisher, editor in chief, superintendent, prime minister, chancellor)
* regularly give press conferences or keynote addresses
* sell expensive items (cruise ships, commercial property, corporations)
* recruit valuable assets for your firm
* represent your company overseas or to foreign clients
* often meet with TT clients or colleagues

AS

SHIRT
Oxford shirt, light blue

TIE
Silk tie, light green

JACKET
Wool jacket, navy

PANTS
Twill pants, light gray

SHOES
Cap-toed oxfords, black leather

YOU MIGHT BE AN "AS" TYPE IF YOU

* work in publishing, marketing, wholesale, retail, health care administration, human resources, nonprofits, higher education, public service, et cetera.
* own a small business

* are an executive at a nontraditional firm
* meet with suppliers, designers, technicians, and other semicasual clients and colleagues
* make calls to companies with semirelaxed dress codes

BB

JACKET
Plaid wool jacket,
oak brown

SHIRT
Blazer shirt, light
indigo blue

BELT
Leather belt,
light brown

PANTS
Wool pants, dark
khaki

SHOES
Penny loafers,
light brown leather

YOU MIGHT BE A "BB" TYPE IF YOU

* work in engineering, manufacturing, academia, or creative industries such as music, film, graphics, architecture, or entertainment
* work in a "creative" department of a corporation
* work at home and go out for meetings and conferences
* are a freelancer
* head up a one- or two-person company
* travel extensively on business and need to look professional, yet still be comfortable
* are a principal at a casual firm

CC

JACKET
Corduroy jacket,
beige

SHIRT
Blazer shirt,
blue-and-white
check

PANTS
Five-pocket
jeans

BELT
Leather belt,
brown

YOU MIGHT BE A "CC" TYPE IF YOU

✳ are a technician, code writer, designer, or other
   expert who has more contact with machines
   than with humans
✳ work in a laboratory
✳ are employed by a laid-back firm where every
   day is casual day

✳ work in an Internet company, especially if it
   was started by people in their twenties
✳ are involved strictly in "back of house"
   operations

THE NEXT STEP

Have you zeroed in on your business casual archetype? Excellent. Your next assignment is to read this book and pay special attention to the outfits and outlines that relate to you and your particular situation.

Not everybody fits neatly into a single category, however.

If you are on the cusp of two or more categories (that is, if your test has resulted in an even score between archetypes, or if there is a slim margin between your highest scores), your wardrobe demands are broader than average and call for creative solutions. For instance, if you have nearly as many points in the Traditional Tailored category as in the Clearly Casual category, you'll need a closetful of comfortable, easy-care ensembles as well as an arsenal of classic trousers, shirts, and blazers. Those of you whose scores straddle Almost a Suit, Best of Both Worlds, and/or Clearly Casual have an easier time of it: Once you understand the essential pieces in each of those categories, it's fairly easy to intensify your level of dressiness or dial it down, as needed.

Now it's time to break the news: Only three of the four types—Almost a Suit, Best of Both Worlds, and Clearly Casual—are addressed in this book. These categories apply to the majority of Americans who contend with casual dress codes at their place of work.

But even if your test results are outside the assigned parameters, you can benefit from knowing the nuances of business casual dressing.

If you've tested as a Traditional Tailored type, and are confronted with casual days at the office, study the Almost a Suit entries for guidance.

SHIRT
Oxford shirt, blue

SWEATER
Cashmere crewneck
sweater, pale green

PANTS
Tailored Twill pants,
light stone

SHOES
Penny loafers,
brown leather

ADVICE

FOR INTERNS, RECENT COLLEGE GRADS, AND ENTRY-LEVEL EMPLOYEES

If you're still in school, or freshly launched from the halls of academia into the cubicles of commerce, the rules of business casual dressing will bend for you . . . to a point. Some corporations show a certain indulgence toward their new hires. It is understood that the young, entry-level—and, in some cases, unpaid—members of their staff are in the midst of a stylistic transition. It isn't easy to go from club kid to copy guy. So, when avant-garde artists become administrative assistants, when ravers appear as receptionists, or when Goths are hired as gofers, there is usually an unspecified (and largely implied) grace period when the junior staffer in question is allowed to incorporate a bit of trendiness or unconventional spunk into the business casual mix.

With that said, please understand that if you are an entry-level employee—just out of school, or not—and you want to succeed, it's a good idea to dress like a grown-up. This doesn't mean you have to squelch your spirit. But if you study the corporate culture of your workplace and figure

out a way to look responsible and appropriate (while maintaining your personal style, of course), you're more likely to gain the trust of your superiors and convince them that you're worthy of promotions, raises, and, when the time comes, positive recommendations to future employers.

Your mission, should you decide to accept it, is threefold. First, identify your current business casual archetype by taking the quiz on page 23. Then, comb through your existing wardrobe and assemble the pieces that could work in your professional environment. Finally, identify any basic elements that you're missing, and acquire them as best you can.

An astute guy in the average entry-level position can mathematically create twenty outfits—enough for one month of workdays—with a wardrobe that consists of three pairs of pants, three shirts, one blazer, and two ties.

And, yes, you'll need shoes, belts, and a whole bunch of socks. But the pieces mentioned in the previous paragraph provide a great starter kit.

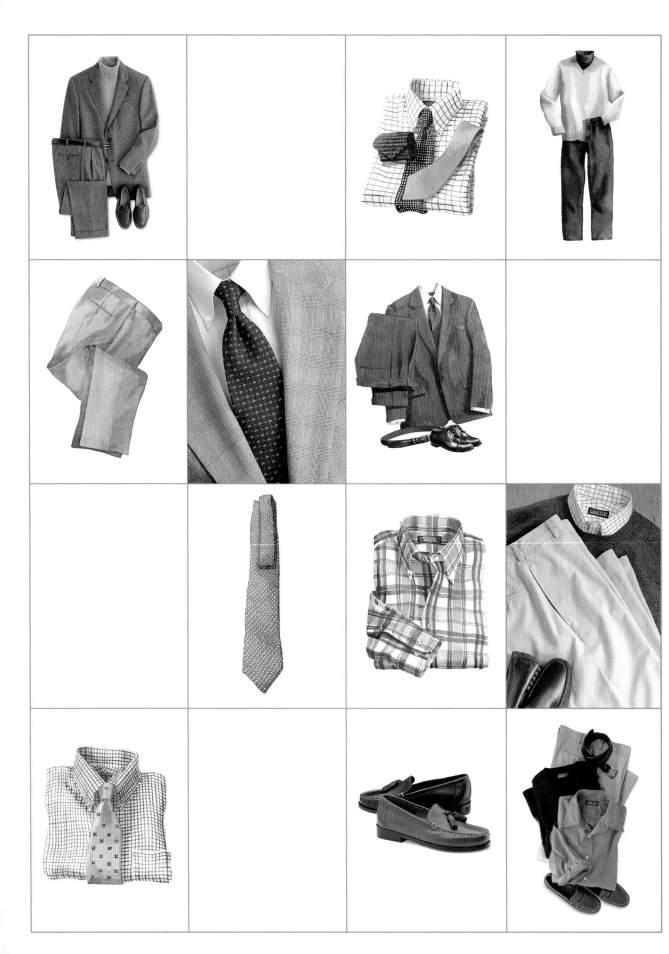

TWO

2
THE LOOKS THAT WORK
A BUSINESS CASUAL PRIMER

There is nothing quite as polished-

looking as a uniform. Firemen have their turnouts. Chauffeurs wear livery. Chefs have their white jackets, checked pants, and tall toques. "I love uniforms," said the decidedly unconventional Andy Warhol in 1977. "It's better to always wear the same thing and know that people are liking you for the real you and not the you your clothes make."

The Traditional Tailored man has a uniform that consists of sharp suits, crisp shirts, and neckties. The business casual man isn't so lucky. His uniforms aren't predetermined, assigned, or doled out in an orderly manner. Rather, they're established on the fly to fit the occasion, with some guidance from informed outsiders. To complicate matters further, the business casual wardrobe is all about flexibility, in more ways than one. If you're like most men, you'll need a number of interchangeable "uniforms" to meet your needs.

Building a casual wardrobe is strictly an à la carte operation; you have to create your own look from pieces chosen from department stores, specialty retailers, catalogs, and more. The ultimate goal is to set yourself up with essential articles of clothing that can be mixed and matched to suit your professional requirements. After reading Chapter 1, you already have a strong idea of how you should look when you go to work. Following is an overview of basic pieces that can work together to define each of the three business casual archetypes.

ALMOST A SUIT ELEMENTS

YEAR'ROUNDER BLAZER, TWO-BUTTON, MIDNIGHT NAVY + BLAZER SHIRT, CLASSIC STRIPE BUTTON-DOWN, BLUE AND WHITE + MINI-DOT TIE, ROYAL BLUE + YEAR'ROUNDER PANTS, PLAIN FRONT, DARK GRAY HEATHER

1. The navy blazer is a perfect stand-in for a traditional suit jacket; it looks polished but lends a slightly rakish air. Here it's paired with charcoal pants—a classic combo—plus a striped button-down shirt and a coordinating tie. Almost a suit, indeed.

THREE-BUTTON SILK-WOOL SPORT COAT, MULTICHECK + LUXURY PINPOINT STRAIGHT-COLLAR SHIRT, CHAMOIS + WOOL-COTTON GABARDINE PANTS, PUTTY + STITCHED CALF-SKIN BELT, ENGLISH TAN + SPLIT-TOED OXFORDS, BROWN

2. A sport coat in shades of brown and tan works wonderfully with earth tones, like putty-colored gabardine pants, a shirt the shade of chamois cloth, and a belt and shoes in basic brown. The overall effect is warm but not wimpy.

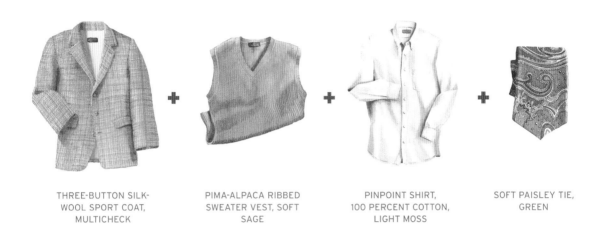

THREE-BUTTON SILK-WOOL SPORT COAT, MULTICHECK

PIMA-ALPACA RIBBED SWEATER VEST, SOFT SAGE

PINPOINT SHIRT, 100 PERCENT COTTON, LIGHT MOSS

SOFT PAISLEY TIE, GREEN

3. Here's that versatile sport coat again, this time paired with a shirt, a sweater vest, and a patterned tie, all in sympathetic shades of green. There's a lot going on, but the tones are all related and so subtle that the outfit hangs together in quite an interesting way.

YEAR'ROUNDER BLAZER, TWO-BUTTON, MIDNIGHT NAVY

LUXURY PINPOINT STRAIGHT-COLLAR SHIRT, CHAMOIS

YEAR'ROUNDER PANTS, PLAIN FRONT, DARK GRAY HEATHER

STITCHED CALFSKIN BELT, BLACK

CAP-TOED OXFORDS, BLACK

4. It's hard to go wrong with a navy blazer and charcoal pants. Usually worn with a white or light blue shirt, here the blazer and pants are softened by a cream-colored shirt tucked into a black belt (and finished at the feet with black oxfords, of course). The tie has disappeared, but with all these classic pieces it's barely missed.

BEST OF BOTH WORLDS BLENDINGS

HOPSACK BLAZER,
THREE-BUTTON,
MIDNIGHT NAVY

BLAZER SHIRT, CHECK
BUTTON-DOWN,
COBALT

EASY-CARE TWILL
PANTS, PLEATED,
BLACK

GLOVE-LEATHER BELT
WITH SILVER BUCKLE,
BLACK

BRUSH-OFF PLAIN-VAMP
LOAFERS,
BLACK

1. Some men prefer a three-button sport coat to a two-button blazer, but both have the same savvy effect. The look is made slightly more casual with a checked blazer shirt in coordinating shades of blue, and black twill trousers topped with a black belt, which coordinates with the polished black loafers.

SILK-LINEN JACKET,
CAMEL

IRISH LINEN
BUTTON-DOWN SHIRT,
FLAX

SOLID REP TIE,
TAUPE

OXFORD-CLOTH
CHINOS,
PALE MAIZE

GLOVE-LEATHER BELT
WITH BRASS BUCKLE,
DARK BROWN

BUCK OXFORDS,
DARK TAN

2. This camel-colored jacket made from a fine blend of silk and linen is great for warmer weather and pairs beautifully with a button-down shirt made of Irish linen. A taupe-toned rep tie adds another layer of subtle color, and the chinos in a classic pale maize shade help give this outfit a stylish, monochromatic look. Brown accessories tie it all together.

BLAZER SHIRT, CHECK
BUTTON-DOWN,
COBALT

BULL'S-EYE ITALIAN
SILK TIE,
BLUE

HOPSACK BLAZER,
THREE-BUTTON,
MIDNIGHT NAVY

CASHMERE CREWNECK
SWEATER,
MERLOT

GLOVE-LEATHER BELT
WITH SILVER BUCKLE,
BLACK

BRUSH-OFF PLAIN-VAMP
LOAFERS,
BLACK

EASY-CARE TWILL
PANTS, PLEATED,
BLACK

3. The navy jacket and checked shirt are layered here with a maroon-colored cashmere crewneck sweater, gussied up with a blue Italian silk necktie. Once again the black pants come into play, as do the black belt and loafers.

SILK-LINEN JACKET,
CAMEL

LONG-SLEEVED PIMA
POLO SHIRT, SOFT
TAUPE

EASY-CARE TWILL
PANTS, PLEATED,
BLACK

GLOVE-LEATHER BELT
WITH SILVER BUCKLE,
BLACK

BRUSH-OFF PLAIN-VAMP
LOAFERS,
BLACK

4. Polo shirts are nice, comfortable options for Best of Both Worlds outfits—however, since they're inherently casual, they benefit from being topped with a sport coat or blazer. Here, a long-sleeved pima polo shirt gets together with the camel jacket, but this time it's matched with black pants and accessories, for a bit of interest.

CLEARLY CASUAL COMBOS

DENIM BLAZER SHIRT,
DEEP WINE

MOCK TURTLENECK,
COTTON,
IVORY

FIVE-POCKET JEANS,
TRADITIONAL, RINSED
DARK INDIGO

BELT WITH SQUARE
SILVER BUCKLE,
BLACK

CASUAL STRAP-BUCKLE
LOAFERS,
BLACK

1. Simple and attractive, this pairing of a deep wine shirt and an ivory-colored turtleneck looks great with traditional five-pocket jeans. To make it office-worthy, the shirt is tucked in and accessorized with a stylish black belt and buckled black loafers.

COMBED-COTTON
CREWNECK SWEATER,
COLONIAL BLUE

MOCK TURTLENECK,
COTTON,
IVORY

CAREFREE CHINOS,
PLAIN FRONT,
GRAY-GREEN

STRETCH SURCINGLE
BELT,
KHAKI

BRUSH-OFF PENNY
LOAFERS,
CORDOVAN

2. The ivory turtleneck peeks out from under a nubby blue cotton sweater, which in turn is layered over chinos. Here, a stretchy belt in a khaki color coordinates well with brown penny loafers.

CASHMERE LONG-SLEEVED
V-NECKED SWEATER,
BLACK

PIMA POLO SHIRT,
HEMMED SLEEVE,
DARK CORAL

FIVE-POCKET JEANS,
TRADITIONAL, RINSED
DARK INDIGO

BELT WITH SQUARE
SILVER BUCKLE,
BLACK

CASUAL STRAP-BUCKLE
LOAFERS,
BLACK

3. A vivid polo shirt in a coral color is sobered up by the addition of a black cashmere sweater, worn with five-pocket jeans and paired with black loafers and a silver-buckled belt. Casual, but chic.

CASHMERE LONG-SLEEVED
V-NECKED SWEATER,
BLACK

T-SHIRT (FOR LAYERING),
SHORT-SLEEVED
CREWNECK, BLACK

CAREFREE CHINOS,
PLAIN FRONT,
GRAY-GREEN

BELT WITH SQUARE
SILVER BUCKLE,
BLACK

CASUAL STRAP-BUCKLE
LOAFERS,
BLACK

4. Once again the black cashmere sweater makes an appearance, but this time a contemporary look is achieved by layering it over a black T-shirt. With neutral-toned chinos, black shoes, and a black belt, the outfit is at once laid-back and sharp.

CRISIS MANAGEMENT

Q: I like being a sharp dresser. Is it possible to follow the rules of business casual and still be on the cutting edge of fashion?

A: Sure. Just don't go overboard.

Example: A skinny knit jersey that's silk-screened with a psychedelic image should probably be reserved for club-hopping. But a designer jacket that anticipates next year's silhouette might work, depending on how you wear it.

Your business casual clothes don't have to be traditional; they only have to be appropriate.

P.S. Steer clear of leather pants, big jewelry, leather vests, radical shoes, enormous belts, and anything made of translucent mesh.

MASTERING THE MYSTERIES OF
COLOR

In the 1960s Broadway musical *Hair,* one number applauded "the male's emergence from his drab camouflage / into the gaudy plumage / which is the birthright of his sex."

The song noted that among most animal species it is the male that displays vibrant feathers and fur. Which seemed a pretty profound observation at a time when men were running around in embroidered Nehru jackets and purple bell-bottoms.

As it turned out, bold colors and flamboyant styles were just a phase. Within a few short years, men faded back into their "drab camouflage" and have been pretty much entrenched in that fashion foxhole ever since.

Whether you're sewn up in a three-piece suit or breathing freely in jeans and a sweater, chances are you're wearing black, gray, brown, white, and/or dark blue. These sober tones may be enlivened by a bright slice of color (in the form of a necktie) now and then, but mostly, men's working wardrobes get their color cues from mud, asphalt, clay, rain clouds, dusk, aspirin, tires, and Band-Aids. A fairly depressing selection, all in all.

One positive aspect of men's limited fashion palette is that, when it comes to mixing and matching colors, it's easy to master the rules.

First, know that dark colors (black, navy blue) are associated with winter and fall but can work year-round, especially in big-city settings. They look dressier (or at least more dangerous) than pale colors or earth tones. Dark trousers and jackets can be paired with almost any shade of shirt or sweater but look especially sharp with white or light-hued shirts and vibrant neckties.

Summery colors such as tan, white, baby blue, yellow, or pink are inherently more casual than dark colors. Accent light-colored pants and jackets with soft, muted, and/or pastel colors, and remember that these shades play best in warm climates, no matter what the season.

Earth tones are in a category all their own. Brown, beige, deep gold, copper, rust, and subtle shades of green (like olive and sage) are casual by nature and work well in virtually any climate or season. Generally speaking, earth tones coordinate well with one another. Avoid pairing them with bright, clear colors such as fire-engine red, taxicab yellow, or vibrant blue.

Now for the shirt/jacket/tie rule: The shirt should be lighter in color than the jacket. The tie should be darker in color than the shirt. Few men can get away with bending this rule.

If you're looking for a foolproof color combo, here it is: Wear a navy blue blazer, a white shirt, charcoal pants, and a bold tie (red, yellow, striped, etc.), and you can't go wrong.

Shoe shades are important. Black shoes go with black, navy, and gray pants; brown shoes go with brown, khaki, and tan pants; cordovan shoes can be worn with brown, gray, and certain dark- to medium-toned blue pants.

In every case, the shoes should match the belt as closely as possible.

As for socks, wear black (or black-based) socks with black shoes and brown (or brownish) socks with brown shoes. Same goes for cordovan and other shades of shoe leather; a close color match looks best. You can also choose to match your socks with your trousers, but remember: Socks don't have to be quite as dark as the shoes, but they should not be lighter or brighter than the pants.

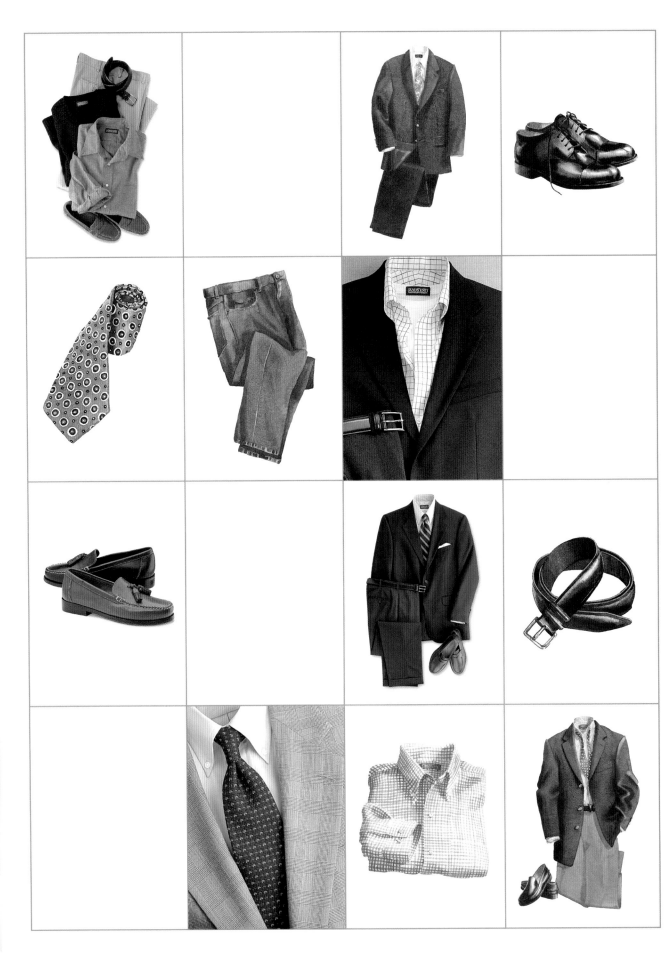

3

THE ELEMENTS OF STYLE

THREE

Jerry Seinfeld once did a stand-up

routine that began with three little words: "I hate clothes." As millions of men in his TV-viewing audience pricked up their ears, he went on to complain about shopping, choosing outfits, and fashion in general. He explained that his personal Utopia, style-wise, was depicted in futuristic movies in which everyone wore the same thing every day: a silver jumpsuit and boots.

Until that sci-fi future comes true, you're stuck with certain realities. Most important is the fact that clothing is both a powerful communicator and an important business tool. People really do "hear with their eyes" and subconsciously judge one another on how they're dressed—especially in professional situations. If you want to make a great impression, you need a great wardrobe. And that means shopping.

This is the part of business casual dressing that most men dread. However, as in football and poker, shopping is much more fun when you know the rules.

You owe it to yourself to develop an educated sense of business fashion. If you start by understanding the basic elements of style, you'll soon be able to spot fine tailoring at fifty paces; detect the difference between a "good" shirt and a shirt that's trying to pass itself off as good; and intuitively put together outfits that are smart and sophisticated, but never stuffy. And along the way, you might even begin to enjoy shopping and choosing clothes.

ALL ABOUT
BLAZERS

The classic navy blazer has a long and much-ballyhooed history. Legend has it that the dark blue, double-breasted jackets, adorned by brass buttons, were first worn by the crew of the H.M.S. *Blazer* at Queen Victoria's coronation. It is said that the queen liked the jackets so much that she made them part of the British Royal Navy uniform. The dark blue color thus became known as navy, a color that has actually been prominent in official naval attire around the world since the eighteenth century.

A second story traces the beginnings of the blazer to the uniforms worn by cricket and rowing teams at English universities. The style and the color were picked up by American Ivy League colleges in the 1920s and soon adopted by country clubs and yachting associations. Along the way, the blazer became a wardrobe staple for American men.

Today's navy blazer might be traditional, with two brass buttons in front and four smaller buttons at each cuff, or it might be an updated version with three dyed-to-match buttons and a longer, more tailored silhouette.

Modern blazers aren't always navy blue, of course. They're available in a tremendous range of fabrics, colors, and patterns. This begs the question: If a blazer-style jacket is made of wheat-colored tweed and has tortoise buttons, is it still called a blazer? Or is the term "sport coat" more accurate?

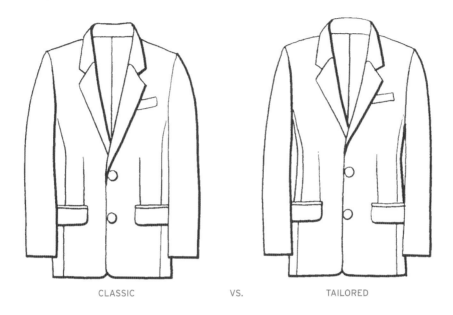

CLASSIC   VS.   TAILORED

In some places, a jacket is considered a blazer if it's a solid color; when it's textured, patterned, or made of a nubby woven material, it's called a sport coat. However, the terms are often interchangeable—and, in fact, so are the pieces.

Blazers and sport coats are the chameleons of the business world. You can wear one with a proper shirt and tie for a take-charge executive look, or pair one with a knit shirt for a more casual statement. Whatever your level of business casual, there is a blazer for you.

Note: The suit jacket, if it's a conservative color like black or navy, can work just like a blazer and be paired with dressy or casual pants, sweaters, and shirts. Try not to dry-clean the jacket more often than the pants so the colors stay matched.

QUINTESSENTIAL BLAZERS

ALMOST A SUIT

BEST OF BOTH WORLDS

Two-button, traditional-fit Year'rounder,
with brass buttons, classic navy

Silk-wool check

CLEARLY CASUAL

Linen, china blue

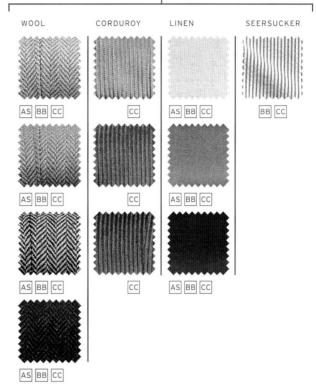

Jackets are a wardrobe basic all year long, but certain patterns and fabrics work better at different times of year and in different settings. Not sure where your jacket belongs? Check the chart above.

Wool (1) and corduroy (2) both work in the cooler months, but while the wool herringbone patterns above are suitable for fall and winter wear for Almost a Suit, Best of Both Worlds, and Clearly Casual guys, the corduroys are in the Clearly Casual camp.

Lightweight linen (3) is perfect for spring and summer in Almost a Suit, Best of Both Worlds, and Clearly Casual wardrobes. Seersucker (4) is wonderfully cooling in summer; it works great for Clearly Casual guys and also can work, with a few dressier touches, in the Best of Both Worlds category.

ALL ABOUT
PANTS

When it comes to business dressing, there are two basic types of trousers: "tailored" and "casual." Your six-year-old daughter might not notice the difference between the two, but it's imperative that you do.

Tailored trousers are commonly known as "dress pants." Usually made of fine fabrics like wool or linen, which drape nicely, they are designed to rest at

a man's natural waistline (unlike casual pants, which ride slightly lower). They feature constructed waistbands fortified by layers of fabric (to anchor them, keep them from rolling, and prevent them from looking crumpled or crushed). Pockets are designed to lie flat against the body and show no bulges from the outside. The best tailored trousers are

DRESS PANTS   TAILORED TROUSERS

PANTS TO AVOID

- Shorts
- Skin-tight pants
- Fleece pants
- Pants intended for sports
- Cargo pants
- Camouflage pants
- Overalls
- Carpenter's pants
- Blue jeans (in most cases)

lined in the crotch and fly area, and wool trousers might be half-lined to the knee. Some styles feature brace buttons (where suspenders can be attached), a watch pocket, and other special details. Most tailored trousers can be easily altered in the length, seat, and waist to achieve a perfect fit.

Casual pants are generally made from sturdy, cotton-based fabrics like twill, corduroy, and denim. They are not lined, and the waistband is made from the same material as the rest of the pant. Happily, most casual trousers can be thrown in the washing machine (unlike tailored pants, which usually require dry-cleaning).

CASUAL PANTS

Design details are what make trousers interesting—and, in some cases, confusing. Here's what you need to know about cuffs and pleats.

∗ Some trousers have five belt loops, which look fine up to a size 32. Beyond that, you'll need seven belt loops.

∗ Deep pockets are a sign of quality and are necessary to avoid the dreaded "pocket dumping" (that's what happens when, due to shallow pockets, you sit down and your possessions land on the floor).

∗ Cuffs are appropriate for most styles of pants, except jeans—unless you're dressing for a 1950s sock hop. Standard cuffs are $1\frac{1}{3}$ inches to $1\frac{5}{8}$ inches deep (the taller you are, the deeper your cuffs can be). Whether you opt for cuffs or not, your pant legs should be long enough that your socks aren't visible while standing or walking.

∗ Once upon a time, pleated pants were considered dressier than plain-front pants. Today, the two styles carry equal weight. Plain-front pants lend a more contemporary look. Pleated pants are quite a bit roomier and are available in double-pleat or triple-pleat styles. If you choose pleats, make sure that they fall in a straight line from the waist to the leg creases. If the pleats gape or spread, you need a larger size or a different style.

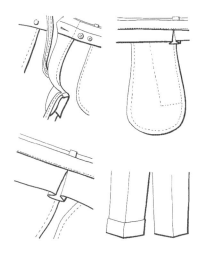

ANATOMY OF A TROUSER

FLAT FRONT   VS.   PLEATED FRONT

SINGLE PLEAT   VS.   DOUBLE PLEAT

QUINTESSENTIAL PANTS

ALMOST A SUIT

BEST OF BOTH WORLDS

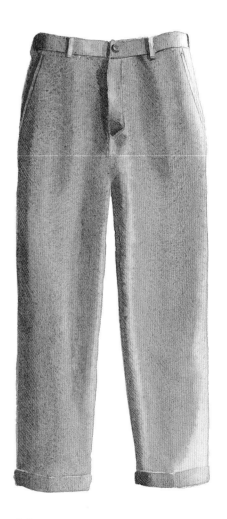

Wool Year'rounders, pleated
front, no cuffs, dark oak

Tailored Twills, flat front,
cuffed, dark fir

CLEARLY CASUAL

Classic pleated-front chinos,
light stone

Generally speaking, the swatches above demonstrate where a fabric falls along the formal/casual continuum. The more formal choices fill the two left-hand columns, moving from dark solid wools at the upper left through patterns and lighter fabrics. The right-hand columns show more casual choices, such as lightweight wools, colorful cottons, and corduroy. For the most part, darker colors, smaller patterns, a finer weave, and wool or wool blends tend toward the more formal end; larger patterns, brighter or lighter colors, and thinner or cotton-based fabrics fall on the casual side. Corduroy may be dark, for instance, but its high cotton content and prominent pattern of wales (vertical ribs) make it Clearly Casual.

JEANS

mericans love jeans. We live in the land of dun-
rees: Those tough, honest trousers represent our
gged individualism, our collective pioneering
rit. We all wear 'em. Grandmas and babies.
wboys and accountants. Rappers, figure
aters, new immigrants, old Yankees. The ques-
n is: Should we wear them to the office?

According to one wide-reaching survey, a whopping 86 percent of
ericans believe that "neat" jeans are appropriate for designated casual
s. Yet a number of tricky issues cling to the jeans question. The biggest
blem is that they're available in a wide range of styles, and not all of
se are office-friendly. Besides the traditional boot-cut or straight-leg
dels with rivets and topstitching, there are oversized hip-hop jeans that
op below the hip line; faded jeans with torn knees; stone-washed jeans
n pleats and cuffs from another era; and jeans emblazoned with promi-
t designer logos—to name only a few.

A second problem is that jeans aren't particularly flattering. Sure, they look great on tall men with slim waists and narrow hips, but the other 90 percent of the population is in danger of looking downright frumpy unless the jeans in question are exactly the right style, shape, and color for them.

Okay, you've been warned. If you're committed to wearing jeans, and are absolutely sure that they're appropriate for your place of business, here are some pointers: First, don't automatically go for the ubiquitous indigo blue. There are all sorts of jeans in shades that range from pale putty to deep black. Find the colors that best suit you and your wardrobe, and be assured that non–blue jeans are good choices for the office, because they read more like casual pants than dungarees. If you can't live without blue blue jeans, steer clear of faded or washed-out shades. The darker the better.

Be aware of your body and its relationship to jeans, and find styles that fit you well and flatter your figure. If you have a prominent belly, wear your jeans with a jacket or long shirt that hides your torso. Length is important. Too long, and they'll look sloppy (and visually shorten your legs); too short, and you'll look like Jed Clampett's cousin. Viewed from the back, your jeans should fall gracefully from the arc of your buttocks and end just above the top of the heel of your shoes, without major bunching or creasing along the way.

When shopping for jeans, don't be tempted by momentary trends. Classic five-pocket jeans are always safe, but if you're tempted to stray from the familiar, go dressier, not more casual. Carpenter jeans or cargo pants could send you into the "dangerously relaxed" zone.

Finally, be sure to update your jeans wardrobe regularly. Favorite dungarees may get softer and more comfy with time, but they're often kept in circulation way past their expiration dates.

ALL ABOUT
SHIRTS

Who could begin to count the numbers of styles, fabrics, colors, and cuts of today's shirts? There are presidential pinpoints and professorial button-downs; there are soft denim shirts and sporty knit polos; there are oxfords and broadcloths and flannels, each with options in collar and cuff styles.

Today, a new breed of shirts is available for the business casual male. Sometimes called "blazer shirts" (because they look good with blazers), these shirts have the personality of a sport shirt with the fit of a dress shirt. The personality comes from the fabrics, which can include denim, corduroy, linen, and lots of cottons in lively checks, stripes, and the like. The fit comes from the tailoring. Unlike most casual shirts, which are sized in an S, M, L, XL format, blazer shirts are made with specific neck and sleeve measurements, just like dress shirts.

Variety is a wonderful thing, but too many choices can cause the casual dresser to go astray. In order to make sense of the vast array of options, it's best to start with a basic understanding of a shirt's relative dressiness. Some general guidelines:

* Long sleeves are appropriate for most every situation, from congressional hearings to PTA meetings.

* Short sleeves are strictly casual and should be reserved for relaxed settings.

* White is the most formal of the solid colors.

* Shirts with subtle stripes and patterns can be worn on their own, dressed up with a suit and a tie, or played down with a sweater.

★ Lively colors and bold prints are more casual than muted solids or quiet patterns.

★ Straight collars are dressier than button-down collars.

★ French cuffs, worn with cuff links, are considered quite formal.

★ The fanciest shirts are made from silky, smooth-finish fabric. Most casual shirts are made from coarser cloth in which the weave can be seen.

★ Popular shirt styles, in more or less descending order from most dressy to least, are broadcloth, pinpoint, oxford, linen, seersucker, denim, pima polo, mesh polo, golf shirt, and T-shirt.

Now that you've absorbed the basic laws of shirts, it's time to get down to the nitty-gritty details.

A SELECTED SHIRT FABRIC GUIDE

COLOR FOR ALL YEAR ROUND

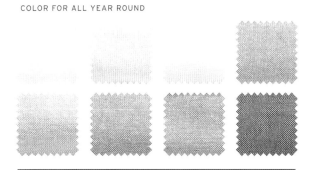

SPECIFICALLY SUMMER WEAR
Searsucker Samples

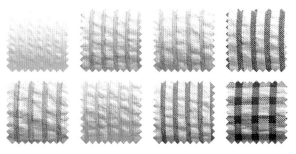

Madras Samples

Most shirt fabrics and colors can be worn year-round. The wearer can decide whether to keep the heavier-weight oxfords for winter or save the brighter colors for summer. Madras and seersucker fabrics, however, are definitely summer wear, whatever their color.

QUINTESSENTIAL SHIRTS

Solid, straight-collar broadcloth,
French cuff, white

Pinpoint, steel gray

Striped button-down
broadcloth, horizon blue

Textured button-down oxford,
two-tone white-and-blue check

Original oxford, honey tan

Pima jersey button-down,
long-sleeved, true blue

QUINTESSENTIAL SHIRTS

CLEARLY CASUAL

Madras, long-sleeved

Pima polo, hemmed short
sleeves, gull gray

Denim blazer shirt, light indigo

SUMMERTIME SHIRTS

You know that shirts made of seersucker and madras are hot-weather favorites. What you might not know is that these fabrics have an underlying logic that is magnificently simple.

Seersucker is a featherweight cotton material that creates a kind of personal air-conditioning system for the body. Its secret? The alternating stripes of flat and crinkly textures assure that just 30 percent of the fabric (the flat areas) touches the skin at any time. If that isn't cool enough, the crinkly stripes absorb excess moisture and wick it away from the body's surface, where it quickly evaporates.

Madras is seersucker's first cousin. Both fabrics originated in India, and both were favored by sweltering British colonists who encountered the subtropical heat there. The distinguishing patterns of madras shirts were inspired by tartan plaids worn by Scottish regiments who occupied India in the 1800s. Local artisans re-created the plaids using their own favorite colors and wove them into loose, breathable cotton textiles.

ALL ABOUT
SWEATERS

The story of the sweater is quite a yarn. (Pause for groans and eye-rolling.)

In the beginning, a "sweater" was a heavy blanket worn by horses. It was designed to make the animals perspire during workouts, which explains the name. These equestrian blankets provided the inspiration for the striped knitted sweaters worn by French sailors. In the 1920s, gentlemen of means began sporting their own versions of the French seamen's style, thus ushering in a new era of comfort and warmth.

True, early sweaters tended to be heavy and itchy and were generally reserved for outdoor activities such as Arctic expeditions. But materials and techniques gradually improved and begot an enormous variety of sweaters so versatile they're practically acrobatic. (Is that why the British call them "jumpers"?)

Knitwear options are many. But not all of them are right for your business casual wardrobe. Banish all thoughts of cable-knit fishermen's sweaters or those droopy cardigans favored by cranky retirees. What you're looking for are fluid jersey crewnecks, fitted sweater vests, cotton-knit turtlenecks, luxuriously soft V necks, or any sweater with a fine-gauge knit. ("Gauge" refers to the thickness of the yarn—fine-gauge yarn is skinny and can be made into lightweight sweaters.)

Fine-gauge sweaters, you'll soon learn, have very little bulk and drape gently on the body. They're perfect for layering on top of a dress shirt (with or without a tie), a polo shirt, a turtleneck, or a T-shirt. They can be worn under a blazer or can stand in for a jacket, turning a plain shirt and pants outfit into a sharp ensemble.

Sweaters add warmth, but you can control the heat by choosing your materials wisely. The coldest weather calls for wool, cashmere, and alpaca sweaters. Cool temperatures in fall and spring are best met with sweaters made of cotton, silk, linen, or Peruvian pima cotton. Merino wool sweaters can be worn in three seasons and have a wonderful feel to them. (In Biblical times, merino sheep were so prized that they were used as currency.)

When shopping for sweaters, expect to come across "blends," which probably feature a combination of natural and synthetic yarns. If easy care is your concern, blended fibers might be your best bet, because the addition of polyester often ensures that a sweater can be machine-washed and still keep its shape—at least for a season or two. The downside is that synthetic-blend sweaters tend to develop "pills" and can become shabby-looking after a number of washings.

In the world of business casual, the way a sweater fits can raise or lower its casual quotient. Generally, the longer the sweater, the slouchier the shoulders, and the more relaxed the neck, the more casual the sweater appears. Seams that fall neatly on one's natural shoulders, sleeves that reach the wrists, and a length that falls at or just slightly below the waist mark a dressier style.

Remember the importance of thickness, too. The finer the gauge, the more professional-looking the sweater. A wide-ribbed cotton knit has an outdoorsy air, and because it's too chunky to showcase a tie or layer under a blazer, it's forever in the Clearly Casual category. A quality cashmere sweater, on the other hand, can qualify as Almost a Suit or Best of Both Worlds, depending on how it's accessorized.

Maybe you think you're not a "sweater guy." That's a shame.

Perhaps the following points will change your mind:

1. In at least half of all business casual situations, a good sweater can substitute for a jacket or blazer and is guaranteed to be more comfortable.

2. Sweaters are soft. Women like touching them.

3. You know that favorite shirt that has an indelible stain on the front? If you wear it under a sweater, no one will know.

4. You know that favorite tie that has an indelible stain on the front? Wear it under a sweater. Your secret will remain safe.

5. Sweaters are flexible in every way and can accommodate many of your moods. For proof, see "1 Sweater, 5 Different Looks," on pages 78 to 79.

1 SWEATER, 5 DIFFERENT LOOKS

Pima fine-gauge V neck, sage green, paired with

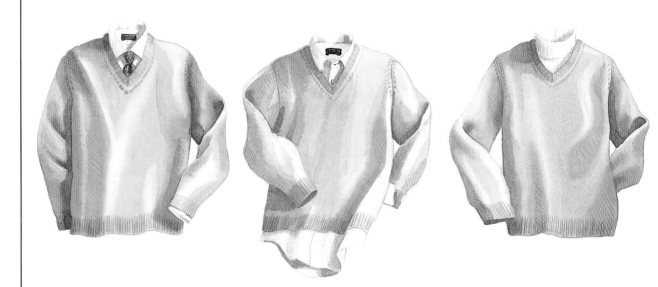

A white, straight-collar broadcloth shirt and light olive "tossed pine" pattern tie

A white oxford button-down shirt

A light sandstone mock turtleneck

From left to right, these combinations illustrate a range from the most formal to the most casual ways to wear a sweater.

A black knit polo shirt

A navy T-shirt

ALL ABOUT
OUTERWEAR

How do you look when you're coming and going? The subject of outerwear is often overlooked when it comes to building a business casual wardrobe. But beware: First impressions are often made when a candidate, client, or colleague comes in from the cold.

As with other elements of style, your outerwear should reflect your level of professionalism as well as your level of casual fashion. Basic outerwear options include the following:

The OVERCOAT: Classic overcoats are made from wool or wool blends and are intended to be worn in chilly weather. They're cut like extra-long blazers (single- or double-breasted), with set-in sleeves, and they range in length from just below the knee to mid-calf. Most are finely tailored and are appropriate for Almost a Suit and Best of Both Worlds wardrobes.

The TRENCH COAT is traditionally a khaki-colored, double-breasted cloth coat that belts at the waist. Most trenches are mid-calf length and are available with or without a warm lining. They're appropriate for all three levels of business casual dressing. *Note:* Unlike the classic tailored overcoat, trench coats have raglan sleeves, which means they fit easily over layers.

The CLASSIC PEA COAT got its style from naval uniforms. It's a short, double-breasted wool jacket that is most often navy blue or black in color. Warm and versatile, it's a nice alternative to synthetic parkas and can be worn by Best of Both Worlds and Clearly Casual men.

The BARN COAT (aka "field coat") is a relaxed, single-breasted, fingertip-length jacket available in heavy cottons, leather, suede, synthetics, and blends. Barn coats are distinguished by oversized patch pockets and short collars, sometimes in contrasting fabrics. Depending on the fabric, a barn coat might be able to squeak into a Best of Both Worlds closet, but more likely it should be reserved for Clearly Casual dressers.

The WINDBREAKER, that staple of golf courses everywhere, is available in a wide range of cuts and fabrics. Though all windbreakers are considered casual, the most Clearly Casual are collarless and have rib-knit trim at the waist and cuffs; the least casual have collars and are finished at the waist and cuffs.

The DENIM JACKET is the most casual of all outerwear. Though solid colors are slightly dressier than classic blue denim, these jackets should be worn only in Clearly Casual situations.

FOUL-WEATHER GEAR (parkas, slickers, etc.) is for foul weather. Nobody wants to freeze or get soaked, but don't mistake foul-weather gear for everyday outerwear.

Zippers Versus Buttons: Maybe it's an old-fashioned notion, but when it comes to outerwear, buttons are dressier than zippers. Therefore, a parka or windbreaker-style jacket gains a few extra points on the formality scale when it has a button-front closure.

The Leather Jacket Question: A well-made, conservatively styled leather or suede jacket is perfectly acceptable as Best of Both Worlds or Clearly Casual outerwear. Avoid motorcycle jackets and parka-style leathers.

Finally, no matter how much you love your authentic New York Yankees parka or your official U2 tour jacket, you should save any logo- or message-emblazoned garb for the weekend.

HATS: It is the rare man who likes wearing hats. Many styles are, frankly, undignified, and even the most fashionable can result in the dreaded condition known as "hat hair." But, whether you love 'em or hate 'em, the day will come when you'll really need a hat to keep you warm and dry. So review your options and choose the right hat before the wrong hat chooses you.

FEDORAS feature a fairly wide brim and a dimpled crown. Dashing and mysterious, they're usually made of felt and look good with trench coats and overcoats; fedoras are also made in fine straw for summer. These hats are recommended for Almost a Suit and Best of Both Worlds types.

DRIVING CAPS are flat-topped hats with short visors, usually made in tweedy, nubby fabrics, that may or may not feature pull-down flaps for winter ear protection. These caps are fine for all three levels of casual.

Simple, knitted WATCH CAPS have two advantages: (1) They can be stuffed in a pocket and pulled out when needed; and (2) they don't often cause hat hair (although they might cause static hair). These caps are suitable for Clearly Casual ensembles.

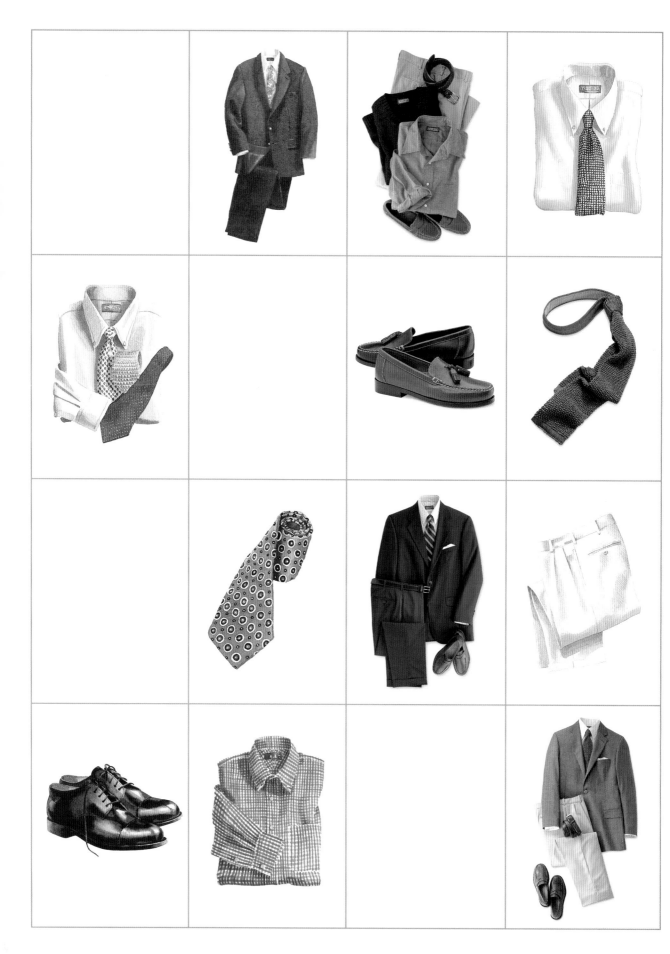

4

ACCESSORIES

FOUR

Little things mean a lot . . . especially

in business casual attire, where ties are tricky, shoes are significant, and belts can make or break a look.

Accessories are the most personal elements of a working wardrobe. Your blazer, shirt, and pants may be straight off the rack and look just like the ones worn by a thousand other guys, but your style—whether you know it or not—is made unique by your choice of wristwatch, cuff links, suspenders, socks, necktie, and so much more (or less, if you're a minimalist).

Don't overlook the details.

Accessories can turn Almost a Suit outfits into Best of Both Worlds ensembles, and vice versa; they can lend an air of propriety to Clearly Casual elements or give Best of Both Worlds a laid-back look. The more you understand the subtle messages sent by accessories, the better dressed you'll be.

squares, and "tossed pine," a pattern of tiny paisley shapes. The *rep* tie (aka "regimental stripe" tie) has strong diagonal stripes and old-boy connotations, as it harkens back to British military regiments. The *grenadine* is a slightly textured silk tie in which the weave of the fabric creates the pattern. The *club* tie usually has a dark background behind a distinct pattern of crests, heraldic symbols, and the like. *Knit* ties are a different animal altogether: They are actually made from knitted material, usually silk. As such, they have a nubby texture and are almost always solid-colored.

DRESS UP OR DRESS DOWN: If you're going for a conservative look, choose ties in solid colors or small patterns. The smaller the pattern—whether it's dots, stripes, windowpane, or paisley—the more formal the tie. In the vernacular of menswear, dark colors are associated with sober, responsible objectives, and neckties are no exception. Ties with bright colors and lighthearted patterns are more casual by nature; most relaxed of all are knit ties, which go well with denim, linen, and other more casual shirts.

THE LONG AND THE SHORT OF IT: Ties, when knotted properly, should fall just to the belt or a tiny bit beyond. Both ends of the tie—the thick and the thin—should be approximately the same length when tied and only slightly overlapped by the wider end. In order to achieve tie perfection, you must start with a tie that is the right length for your body. Today's standard tie lengths are 57 inches (regular) and 61 inches (long). Unless you have unusual proportions, one of these lengths should work for you. It is important that you experiment in front of a mirror to find your proper tie size; an overly long tie can look messy, while a too-short tie flatters no man.

THROUGH THICK AND THIN: In 1967, Ralph Lauren shocked the fashion world (and launched his career) by introducing a tie that was three inches wide. Throughout the previous decade, neckties were a skinny two inches across, but Lauren had started a craze for width that peaked in the 1970s, when ties were so wide they could double as bibs (and often did). Today, the widest part (the "apron") of a classic tie is 3.5 inches, give or take a quarter inch.

A KNOTTY SUBJECT: Oscar Wilde once said, "A well-tied tie is the first serious step in life." Your well-knotted tie should nestle comfortably under the collar, without causing it to splay out on either side, and feature a crisp dimple in the center just below the knot.

The standard American knot is the *four-in-hand*, which takes its name from a British horse-drawn coach. It is the simplest, smallest, and flattest of knots, and it's probably the one that you learned to tie in front of the bathroom mirror when you were fourteen. More complicated knots are the *Windsor*, a thick and tricky arrangement made popular by the Duke of Windsor; and the *half-Windsor*, a wide but less-bulky knot, suitable for spread-style collars.

QUALITY CONTROL: To test the quality of a necktie, drape the narrow part across your hand and hold the tie in the air. If the dangling section begins to twist—a phenomenon known as "corkscrewing"—it hasn't been properly cut and doesn't belong in your wardrobe. Next, examine the underside of the tie. At the point where the two ends of fabric come together to form an inverted V, you should see a stitch joining the flaps. This is the "bar tack." It helps maintain the shape of the tie and is the sign of a well-made piece of neckwear.

SEVEN PLEAT

NEWS FLASH: Did you know that there's a new knot in town? It was adopted by the Neckware Association of America in the late 1980s—and it was the first new knot the association had heard of in fifty years. Called the *Pratt Knot*, it was invented by American businessman Jerry Pratt. The knot received widespread coverage in 1989 when a Minneapolis anchorman named Don Shelby featured it on TV. The story was picked up by the international press, who mistakenly dubbed it the Shelby Knot. In any case, it's an unorthodox knot because it starts with the tie inside-out. When the knot is completed, however, you end up with a slim, tidy knot that sits well and looks good.

TO TIE A PRATT, OR SHELBY, KNOT

1. Place the tie around your neck "inside out," with the pattern facing toward the neck. The front of the tie (the thick end) should be underneath and facing inward.

2. Pull the thick end of the tie up and through the neck loop. Continue to pull this end down.

3. Pull the loop down and tighten.

4. Pull the thick end of the tie to the left with your left hand.

5. Pull the thick end behind the neck loop and then up, preparing for the finish.

6. Pull the front of the tie down through the tuck and gently tighten.

The resulting knot should be smaller than a Windsor but slightly larger than a traditional tie knot.

ADVENTUROUS ALTERNATIVES: It's fun to wear a *novelty-print tie* once in a while, but if you want respect, stick with holiday-themed ties and wear them *only* on the holiday in question. *Bow ties* are rarely successful in the business world; unless the bow tie is your signature look (and it looks good on you), you should save your bow ties for when you're wearing a tuxedo. *Ascots* and *scarves* are likewise considered to be formal wear. Some men feel better dressed when they match their necktie to a *pocket square,* and indeed, the right pocket square–tie combo can brighten up a sober suit. Be aware that shiny or loud-print pocket squares and ties may be considered odd, but it's perfectly okay to wear a modest pocket square, with or without a tie, for a creative casual look.

CRISIS MANAGEMENT

Q: I've heard that, in order to get ahead, I should dress like my boss. The problem is that my boss wears suits, and everyone else in my department wears jeans and sneakers. How do I get noticed by the authority figure without alienating my colleagues?

A: The solution you seek can be found via compromise. You're smart to echo your boss's style. It's the sincerest form of flattery and sets you up for positive recognition, both personal and professional. And yet, the acceptance of your peers might also be important to your success, not to mention avoiding the perception of being a brownnoser.

Business casual is your answer. You don't need to wear a three-piece suit to get noticed, especially when your outfit is being viewed in contrast to your coworkers' jeans and sneakers. All you really need to do is dial the dressiness up a notch or two. Try polo shirts and chinos; wear leather shoes; tuck a necktie under a V-necked sweater; and don a blazer now and then.

When in doubt, remember what Benjamin Franklin once said: "Eat to please yourself, but dress to please others."

ALL ABOUT
SHOES

The importance of shoes is reflected in our language: A prosperous person is known as "well-heeled," while less-fortunate souls are "run down at the heels." And, although Frank Zappa once declared that "brown shoes don't make it," just about any style or color of shoes makes it in business casual—as long as the shoes in question are leather and, yes, well-heeled.

SHOES TO AVOID

Among the shoe styles that shouldn't set foot in the office:

- Athletic shoes
- Deck shoes
- Boots including fashion boots, work boots, hiking boots, desert boots, and cowboy boots
- Sandals

WALK LIKE A MAN: Until casual fever caught on in offices, the proper corporate shoe was the lace-up oxford—with or without a perforated toe—in black, dark brown, or cordovan. Soles were leather, and uppers were always shined. Today, men's business casual options include buckle loafers, tassel loafers, penny loafers, driving shoes, and even suede bucks.

Oxfords and wing tips are the dressiest of the business shoes, but they still have their place in relaxed wardrobes. Loafers are less dressy, while nub-soled driving moccasins are about the most casual shoe that you can get away with at the office.

When judging the casual quotient of a shoe, there are many factors to consider, and each is relative to another. Using the guidelines shown below and on the opposite page, you can safely conclude that the most casual shoes would be moccasin-style loafers with nubby rubber soles, and the dressiest shoes would be shiny black oxfords with leather soles and heels. Somewhere in between is a brown penny loafer made from pebble-grain leather.

CASUAL QUOTIENT

LACE-UPS = DRESSIER	SLIP-ONS = MORE CASUAL	LEATHER SOLES = DRESSIER	RUBBER SOLES = MORE CASUAL	THICK OR TEXTURED RUBBER SOLES = MOST CASUAL

Shoe styles fall on a continuum from dressy lace-up oxfords with a smooth finish (left) to more casual, but still office-worthy penny loafers (right). Generally, lace-ups, leather soles, and tassels mark more formal styles; rubber soles, penny loafers, and plain tops indicate more casual wear.

Textured soles on moccasin-style loafers make these shoes much more casual than those above, but even then subtle variations in style and texture make some, such as the smooth penny loafers on the far right, dressier than others, such as the suede plain-topped moccasins, third from the left.

| TASSEL LOAFERS =
DRESSIER | PLAIN-TOP LOAFERS =
DRESSIER | PENNY LOAFERS =
MORE CASUAL | FLAT-SOLED MOCCASIN-
STYLE LOAFERS =
MOST CASUAL |

CRACKING THE COLOR CODE: Shoe colors have strange names. Sure, you know what brown and black look like. Here's a quick review of the more mysterious shades.

CORDOVAN =
REDDISH BROWN

OXBLOOD =
REDDISH BLACK

DARK ENGLISH TAN =
NOT QUITE AS DARK AS
BROWN BUT DARKER THAN
TAN, WITH REDDISH
HIGHLIGHTS

Now that you know your colors, it's time to learn the rules of shoe/trouser/belt/socks coordination:

* The shoes must match the belt.

* Black shoes go with black, navy, and gray pants.

* Brown shoes go with brown, khaki, gray, blue, and navy pants.

* Cordovan shoes can be worn with brown, gray, and navy pants.

* Wear black (or black-based) socks with black shoes and brown (or brownish) socks with brown shoes. Same goes for cordovan and other shades of leather; a close color match looks best.

* You can also match your socks to your pant color, as long as they're no lighter than the pant color.

* Thin socks are dressy. Thick socks are not.

* Small patterns on a sock are dressier than large patterns (argyle being definitely casual).

THE QUALITY EQUATION

Cheap shoes are rarely a bargain. Why? Because most low-priced shoes are made from synthetic materials, which (1) don't expand, and therefore will never "break in" to accommodate your foot; (2) make your feet perspire, which is miserable in any season; and (3) wear badly and can't be polished successfully. Even when an inexpensive shoe is made of leather, its low price usually indicates inferior stitching and construction. Cheap shoes almost always look cheap. High-quality footwear, made of natural materials and constructed by artisans, may cost more up front but will pay for itself in comfort, longevity, and good looks.

QUINTESSENTIAL SHOES

ALMOST A SUIT

Cap-toed oxfords

BEST OF BOTH WORLDS

Tassel loafers

Classic penny loafers

Flexible-soled penny loafers

CLEARLY CASUAL

Driving mocs

ALL ABOUT
BELTS

Belts not only hold up your pants, but they can also help shore up your reputation. Like shoes, belts hold certain places in the business casual hierarchy. But no matter what their level of formality, they should always be made (at least partially) of genuine leather.

BLACK LEATHER BELT =
DRESSIER

CONTRASTED TOP-STITCHING =
MORE CASUAL

FABRIC OR SURCINGLE BELT =
MOST CASUAL

COLORS AND MATERIAL

Black leather = dressier

Brown leather = more casual

Tan leather = more casual

Fabric = most casual

FINISHES

Smooth, shiny leather = dressier

Embossed hide texture (crocodile, snakeskin) = dressier

Dull texture (pebble-grain, suede, nubuck) = more casual

Contrasted top-stitching = more casual

Braided leather = more casual

Fabric or surcingle belt = most casual

FINISH OF BUCKLE

Shiny buckle = dressier

Matte buckle = more casual

STYLE OF BUCKLE

Slim buckle = dressier

Chunky buckle = more casual

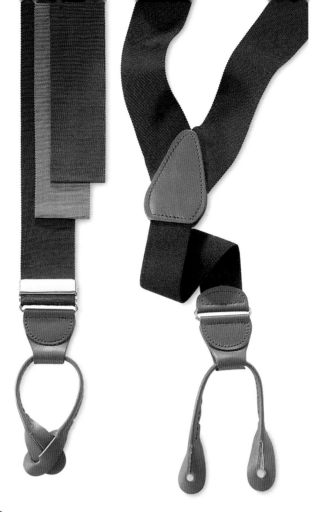

SUSPENDERS

Whether you call them "suspenders" or "braces," they'll shoulder the burden of holding up your pants. Like bow ties and cravats, suspenders are a specialized accessory that work for some—but not all—men. What's more, they're considered to be highly traditional and don't blend all that well into the business casual landscape.

Here are a few things you need to know about braces:

✴ Proper braces attach to the pants via leather tabs. These tabs hook into six buttons on the waistband of the trousers: two in back and four in front on either side of the fly.

✴ Avoid wearing suspenders that attach to the pants via clips.

✴ The leather tabs should match your shoes (i.e., don't wear brown-tabbed braces with black shoes, and vice versa).

✴ If you have a protruding stomach—even a *slightly* protruding stomach—suspenders are not flattering.

✴ Steer clear of suspenders in silly colors or patterns.

ALL ABOUT
BUSINESS CASES

No man is without stuff: stuff that needs to be carried around; stuff you've got to have to do your job; stuff that seems to expand exponentially every year. Your father might have been well served by a standard attaché case, in which he probably stashed files, a datebook, a leather folder full of business cards, a picture of your mother, and a calculator . . . but what are your needs? As a modern man of business, it's your job to take inventory of the gear you routinely shuttle from place to place and to find a business case (or two) that can accommodate your unique requirements.

STEP 1

Make a list of the minimum amount of equipment you commute with on a day-to-day basis. Inventory basic items like your cell phone, keys, Palm Pilot, pager, train schedules, disks, asthma inhaler, legal pads, sunglasses, pens, and so forth.

STEP 2

Count the maximum number of items you'll ever need to bring to work. Include a laptop computer, product samples, spare shoes, a portable stereo, CDs, an umbrella, lunch, bound reports, file folders, a digital camera, contact lens solution, et cetera.

With inventories in hand, decide whether you need (1) one small, streamlined case, just big enough to carry your essentials; (2) a small case to carry every day, plus a larger case to tote when duty calls; or (3) a large case to carry every day.

Business cases come in many shapes and sizes, some more casual than others.

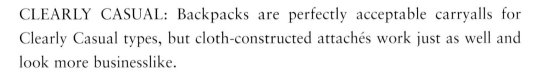

ALMOST A SUIT: A leather attaché case, either soft-sided or hard-shelled, works best for men who regularly encounter traditional clients or associates. Choose a slim case if you tend to travel light and a deeper, expandable case if you're usually loaded down. If you commute by train or bus, keep in mind that a hard-sided case makes a great portable desk.

BEST OF BOTH WORLDS: "Stuffable" attaché cases made of nylon, cotton, or supple leather are lighter and more flexible than traditional cases and work beautifully in a wide range of business situations. In addition, many have shoulder straps, making them more comfortable to carry.

CLEARLY CASUAL: Backpacks are perfectly acceptable carryalls for Clearly Casual types, but cloth-constructed attachés work just as well and look more businesslike.

YOUR PRIVATE CELL

Don't imagine that your cell phone is a fashion accessory. Okay, it's probably way cool, with an iridescent face and functions that George Jetson never dreamed of, and it might even play a downloaded version of "Comfortably Numb" whenever someone calls.

✳ Nevertheless, a cell phone is not an article of clothing, a piece of jewelry, or a bauble to be displayed on your belt or anywhere else.

✳ Keep the phone in your pocket or in your business case, please. And turn off that ringer when you're at work. Can you hear me now?

WHAT TO PACK FOR A
THREE-DAY BUSINESS TRIP

The problem with packing for business casual trips is that you don't really know how to dress until you get there. The best fashion strategy is to plan a flexible wardrobe that might be a bit dressier than is really necessary but definitely won't be too casual. After all, you don't want to be wearing the only polo shirt and chinos in a sea of dark suits.

The following packing template works for Almost a Suit and Best of Both Worlds archetypes. With a few adjustments, it can also serve as a guide for Clearly Casual travelers.

WHAT YOU NEED

☐ One navy blazer

☐ One pair of gray (or "charcoal") tailored trousers

☐ One pair of casual trousers (i.e., chinos) in a dark khaki color

☐ Three shirts: (1) a light blue shirt, with a button-down collar; (2) a blue-and-white striped shirt, with a straight collar; and (3) a long-sleeved polo shirt in an off-white shade (heather, ivory, tan, chamois)

☐ One V-necked or cardigan sweater in red or green

☐ A couple of neckties. One should have navy as its dominant color; the other should be predominantly red (to coordinate with your sweater, if needed).

☐ Two pairs of leather shoes: one black, one brown. Lace-ups or polished loafers will be fine. You may want to bring a third pair of shamelessly comfortable shoes to keep your feet happy while you sprint through airports or go on walking tours. Remember: Sneakers or athletic shoes are not advised for professional situations, especially in major cities or anywhere in Europe.

☐ Four pairs of thin dress socks: two black, two brown. Go ahead and sneak in a cushy pair of athletic socks for when you're strolling around in your nonbusiness shoes.

☐ One black and one brown belt

☐ Appropriate outerwear for the climate and the season

☐ Underwear, sleepwear, and clothes to hit the town in after-hours

PUTTING IT ALL TOGETHER

DAY 1

Until you're sure of your client's level of business casual, it's best to dress to impress. Wear:

* Navy blazer
* Blue button-collar shirt
* Gray dress trousers
* Neutral tie
* Black shoes and socks

DAY 2

Assuming you've made an impression and are slightly more relaxed (in keeping with your client and his or her company's style, of course), try:

* Green sweater
* Gray dress trousers
* Blue-and-white striped shirt
* Black shoes and socks

DAY 3

By now, you've established yourself as a key player. Your clothes, though still important, are secondary to your talents, skills, and personality. Are you ready to ditch the tie and get down to some serious work? Dress in:

* Blue shirt
* Khaki-colored chinos
* Brown shoes and socks
* Brown belt

ALTERNATIVE OUTFITS

You can adjust your level of casual comfort as business situations unfold. Some alternative ensembles include:

- [ ] Navy blazer
- [ ] Blue-and-white striped shirt
- [ ] Khaki-colored chinos
- [ ] Brown shoes and socks
- [ ] Brown belt

- [ ] Red sweater
- [ ] Long-sleeved, off-white polo shirt
- [ ] Khaki-colored chinos
- [ ] Brown shoes and socks
- [ ] Brown belt

- [ ] Green sweater
- [ ] Striped shirt
- [ ] Blue tie
- [ ] Gray dress trousers
- [ ] Black shoes and socks
- [ ] Black belt

- [ ] Long-sleeved, off-white polo shirt
- [ ] Khaki-colored chinos
- [ ] Brown shoes and socks
- [ ] Brown belt

5
THE PROPER FIT

FIVE

"Know, first, who you are; and then

adorn yourself accordingly." When Epictetus wrote these words in A.D. 100, he was undoubtedly referring to knowing one's soul. But his wisdom can also apply to the body.

Statistics show that first impressions are made in about 80 seconds. Within that tiny sliver of time, the people you meet take a mental snapshot and size up your style, personal hygiene, body language, speech patterns, and the appropriateness of your attire. It's been shown that even the most sympathetic strangers can't help but make snap "capability" judgments based on their visual impressions.

So what does this have to do with the fit of your clothes? Plenty.

An ill-fitting outfit—no matter how carefully you choose it or how much money you spend on it—is going to work against you. If any of your pants, shirts, or jackets are too big and/or too long, they're going to make you look sloppy, flabby, or unkempt. When the same pieces are tight and/or short, you risk looking gangly, geeky, or pudgy.

Before you start your quest for a good fit, however, it's important that you understand what does or does not flatter your body. Whether you're built like Michael Jordan or more like George Costanza, there are styles and shapes that will flatter you. Likewise, there are styles and shapes that you should learn to avoid.

HOW TO
FLATTER YOURSELF

If you have a perfect body, please disregard the following section and move on to "Finding Your Fit," on page 126.

The other 99.9 percent of you should read on, and keep in mind that, whatever your level of business casual, you can develop an individual style that accentuates the positive and camouflages the negative.

Men's figure negatives generally fall into four broad categories: too heavy, too short, too slim, or too tall. Conveniently enough, the styles that flatter bulky men tend to be good choices for men who wish they were taller. Similarly, men who are unusually lean look their best in the very same clothes that complement those who are extra tall.

HOW TO
DISGUISE EXCESS WEIGHT

The right clothes can visually stretch the body, making it seem longer and narrower than it really is. The trick here is to employ strong vertical lines, while downplaying horizontal elements (especially along the belt line). Some tips:

AVOID WEARING WHITE (OR LIGHT-COLORED) SHIRTS WITH DARK TROUSERS. A dramatic contrast between your shirt and pants will draw the eye to the midriff area, which is bad news for heavier men because it articulates their width. To counteract this, choose a shirt and a belt that are similar in color and tone to your trousers. This will help create an unbroken line from your ankles to your neck.

A BLAZER (OR SPORT COAT) IS YOUR BEST FRIEND. Why? Because it creates an attractive silhouette in which the shoulders are exaggerated and the torso is hidden under smooth, structured expanses of cloth. The fuller, two-button American cut is advised here.

CHOOSE TO GO TIELESS, WHEN YOU CAN. Big men with thick necks can look strangled in traditional shirt-and-tie combos; the alternative is an open collar, a button-down collar, or a V-necked sweater.

AND WHEN YOU CAN'T . . . That's okay, too. A necktie makes a flattering vertical connection between your belt and your collar. Its benefits are twofold: First, it acts as a kind of racing stripe, making your torso seem longer and more sleek. Second, it covers the buttons on your shirt, which is a real blessing if you've had an indulgent lunch.

GIVE CUFFS THE BOOT. Cuffs are a horizontal element . . . and that means they steal height and add weight. Cuff-free pants, sometimes known as "plain-bottomed," are for you.

ALMOST A SUIT ELEMENTS

JACKET
Linen-cotton sport
coat, dark navy

TIE
Printed paisley
tie, maize

SHIRT
Pinpoint solid shirt,
light chamois

PANTS
Original gabardines,
plain front, no cuffs,
midnight navy

CLEARLY CASUAL COMBOS

PANTS
Classic jeans, khaki

SHIRT
Peruvian pima polo shirt, hemmed, short-sleeved, black

HOW TO
ADD HEIGHT

Yes, you really can fool the eye and make yourself appear taller. All it takes are some savvy style choices. Here's how:

AVOID HIGH CONTRAST BETWEEN YOUR SHIRT AND TROUSERS. A dramatic contrast between top and bottom—say, a white shirt and black pants—draws the eye to the waistline, which can visually cut you in half. To counteract this, choose a shirt and a belt that are similar in color or tone to your trousers.

A BLAZER (OR SPORT COAT) ADDS LENGTH. No matter what their girth, height-challenged men are complemented by the long lapels and high shoulders of blazers. If you're slim or medium around the waist, the trim, three-buttoned "new tailored" cut is advised here. Wider men should stick with the traditional American cut. Whichever you choose, make sure that the length of the body of the jacket does not extend beyond your fingertips.

GO WITH THE TIE. A necktie makes a flattering stripe between your belt and your collar and can help make your torso seem longer. Highly contrasting ties and shirts are a good look for you.

SAY NO TO CUFFED TROUSERS. Cuff-free pants, sometimes known as "plain-bottomed," are most flattering to not-tall men.

BEST OF BOTH WORLDS BLENDINGS

SHIRT
Blazer shirt,
striped button-down,
dark pink

JACKET
Wool blazer,
midnight navy

PANTS
Easy-care twills,
plain front,
midnight navy

ALMOST A SUIT ELEMENTS

TIE
Italian silk tie,
sand

JACKET
Two-button silk-wool
sport coat, tan

SHIRT
Irish linen shirt, pale
blue plaid

PANTS
Year'rounder pants,
pleated, camel heather

HOW TO
BULK UP A SLIM FRAME AND/OR DIMINISH YOUR HEIGHT

Tall, slim guys usually look great in clothes and are the envy of many a 48 Short. But the man who is unusually tall has his own set of business casual challenges, and so does his colleague who is especially narrow. Both have the same mission when it comes to dressing their best: Emphasize width and abbreviate height. Here's how:

WEAR SWEATERS. Crewnecks, ribbed knits, turtlenecks, sweater vests, and cardigans are all excellent choices for men who are tall and/or slim. They not only bulk up the torso but also create a line of contrast near the waist. The result is an illusion of more weight and less height. P.S. If you're especially lean, go ahead and tuck your sweater into your pants (unless it's a vest or a cardigan, of course).

GO HORIZONTAL. You can choose heavy belts, horizontally striped jerseys, shirts with contrasting collars . . . anything that draws the eye from left to right, and back again. When it comes to dress shirts, which rarely feature horizontal stripes, opt for checked, windowpane, or plaid patterns and avoid those with vertical striping.

DRESS IN LAYERS. Season permitting, button a vest over a turtleneck jersey, and top it with a sport coat. Wear a substantial T-shirt under a denim shirt. Thread a tie through the collar of an oxford shirt, add a V-necked sweater, and finish the look with a blazer. The more layers, the more balanced your proportions will look.

HAVE FUN WITH CONTRASTS. You can make yourself seem broader with contrasting colors. Try an orange shirt with navy trousers; a forest-green polo with khaki pants; a cream-colored sweater with black chinos; or any combination that pitches dark tones against bright. Contrasting colors usually collide along the waistline, which creates a point of interest that complements men who are tall and/or slim.

TALL MEN NEED LONG BLAZERS. If you're over six feet tall, you'll look better when your blazer or sport coat is hemmed an inch or so below your fingertips—no matter if you're built like a barrel-chested linebacker or are as lean as a long-distance runner. *Note:* Those of you who are underweight but not particularly tall should stick with traditional-length blazers.

CHOOSE PLEATED PANTS. Single- or double-pleated pants are ideal choices for the lean and the lanky. That's because they tend to spread extra fabric over the thigh and hip areas, thus creating a broader silhouette that gives the impression of added width.

CUFF 'EM. Men with long legs look great in cuffed pants. Why? Because cuffs make trousers—and the legs that fill them—seem shorter and draw attention to the shoes rather than the calves.

FINDING YOUR FIT

Now that we've explored the subtleties of shapes, it's time to do the math that will add up to your proper fit. Do you have a tape measure ready? Good. The sizing of men's attire may at first appear to be as abstract as Chinese algebra, but all the numbers eventually conspire to identify sizes that make you look great. The best, most accurate, thing to do is to have a salesperson at a reputable men's store or men's department do this for you.

SHIRTS

Men's shirt sizes are a combination of collar and sleeve measurements. A 17/35 shirt, for instance, features a 17-inch collar and a 35-inch sleeve. Here's how to identify your individual shirt size:

✶ First, measure around the lowest part of your neck. Place two fingers between the tape and your neck, then round off to the nearest half inch. This is your collar size.

✶ Put one hand on your hip. Starting from the center of your back, just below the neck, measure out to your shoulder. Continue down to your elbow, all the way to one inch or so below your wrist. The total number of these inches is your proper sleeve length.

JACKETS, BLAZERS, AND SPORT COATS

Jacket sizes are based on the circumference of the chest. There are two ways to accurately measure your chest:

* The traditional method is to place a tape measure under your arms and around your chest, at its fullest point. Insert one finger under the tape. This equals your proper jacket size.

* An alternative method, which is more accurate if you have big, muscular arms, is to put your arms at your sides and have a friend run the tape measure across the outside of your arms and across the fullest part of your chest. Subtract six inches. This is your jacket size.

Now that you know your jacket size (which is also your suit size, but please see "Suits," on page 129, for specifics), here are some details to look for when choosing a style:

* The collar of your jacket should hug the back of the neck, without buckling or pulling, and should expose a half inch of the shirt collar in the back.

* Lapels should lie flat on your chest, without buckling.

* Most jackets and blazers feature two or three buttons, and the placement of these buttons may either be "high stance" (positioned higher on the front of the suit, below shorter lapels) or "low stance" (lower on the suit, below longer lapels.) If you have wide shoulders and slimmer hips, go for "low stance"; if you tend to have a belly, a "high stance" is more flattering for you.

* Sleeves should end just below your wrist bone and show a quarter inch or so of your shirtsleeve.

* Some jackets have one or two vents, which are flaps of cloth below the waist in the back, and which allow freedom of movement. Men with prominent or wide posteriors should choose two flaps. If you're medium in the back, choose one; if you're slim where you sit, you may choose a jacket with no flaps at all.

PANTS

As with shirts, pant sizes are gauged both in width and length (i.e., waist and inseam). For example, a 38/34 pant fits a man with a 38-inch waist and a 34-inch inseam. To find your size:

✳ First, measure around your waist at the point where you normally wear your pants. Keep one finger between the tape and your body. Voilà. Another way to make this calculation is to run a tape measure along the waistline of your most comfortable pants.

✳ To calculate your inseam, you can measure yourself from the crotch to the inside of your ankle, but it's much easier to measure the length of your best-fitting trousers. Again, you'll be running the tape from the crotch seam to the inside bottom edge of the pants.

✳ The perfect-length pant should "break" softly about a quarter inch over the shoe and should cover about two-thirds of the shoe, with the back of the hem hitting just above the heel. Dress trousers are usually custom-hemmed; if you're ordering by mail or via the Internet, it's important that you measure some trousers you own that meet these requirements.

DIVIDE AND CONQUER

If you're hard to fit, you'll be glad to know that certain enlightened retailers are now selling suits as separate pieces—that is, you can purchase the jacket in your size and the pants in your size. This is good news for men who wear, say, a size 48 jacket and a size 38 pants.

✳ "Rise" is the distance between your waist and the crotch seam. If you're over six feet tall, you'll be more comfortable in pants that feature a "long rise."

✳ Cuffs, if you choose to wear them, should be 1 to 1.5 inches deep.

BELTS

These are based on waist measurements, but are usually offered in even sizes only, so round up if your waist size happens to be an odd number.

MEN'S SIZING CHART

	SMALL		MEDIUM		LARGE		X-LARGE		XXL	
TOPS										
NECK	14	14 ½	15	15 ½	16	16 ½	17	17 ½	18	18 ½
CHEST	34	36	38	40	42	44	46	48	50	52
ARM (reg.)	32 ½	33	33 ½	34	34 ½	35	35 ½	36	36 ½	36 ½
ARM (tall)	34	34 ½	35	35 ½	36	36 ½	37	37 ½	38	38
BOTTOMS										
WAIST	28	30	32	34	36	38	40	42	44	46
HIP	34	36	38	40	42	44	45 ½	47	48 ½	50 ¼

SWEATERS, POLO SHIRTS, AND OTHER KNITS

These are usually sized Small, Medium, Large, et cetera. If you're not sure where you fit in, check the chart above.

SUITS

Your suit size is the same as your jacket size, with the added variable of Short, Regular, or Long. The size of suit pants are standardized and are based on chest measurements minus six inches (for suit sizes up to 46) or five inches (for sizes 48 and up).

For instance, if you order a size 42 suit (based on your chest/jacket size), it will come with 36-inch-waist trousers. If your suit size is 51, the pants that come with your suit will have a 46-inch waist.

ALTERED
STATES

Some wealthy men have their suits, jackets, and trousers custom-made for them. The measurements used to create these clothes are exhaustive and precise; that's one reason why the elite can seem so effortlessly fashionable, even if they have imperfect bodies.

So how can you achieve a faultless fit? Today, with the magic of a new computerized cutting machine, custom clothes can be made for you at surprisingly affordable prices. Usually, these services are either phone- or Web-based—that is, you tell your measurements to a customer rep or enter your measurements into an order form on the Internet. You also give your preferences for styles, colors, fabrics, et cetera. These numbers are fed into a machine that custom-cuts the panels that make up your clothes. Your new duds are then hemmed to your specifications and shipped to you, ready to wear. As an added bonus, your measurements are stored for future use, so the next time you need, say, a pair of trousers that rest perfectly around your hips and don't get "smile lines" in the crotch area, all you need to do is make a quick phone call or get on the Internet with your customer ID code. A number of better clothing companies—including Lands' End—now offer these services. They're a real godsend, especially for men who live in remote areas or have hard-to-fit bodies, or both.

The old-fashioned tailor still has an important place in the world, however. You can find one at virtually every decent men's shop or department store. Here, in-store tailors will do basic alterations (e.g., hemming trousers and cuffs). If your body falls outside the perimeters of standard sizes, you can either book additional fittings with the store's tailor or visit an independent tailor shop on your own.

Like a talented mechanic or a reliable plumber, a good tailor is a friend for life. As long as the clothes you wish to alter are high-quality—and we hope, if you've been reading this book, you know by now how important that is—alterations are worth every penny.

6
WARDROBE MAINTENANCE

Business casual clothes are easy on

the eyes, easy on the wallet, and easy on the body. What more could you ask from your wardrobe?

How about easy care? Nine out of ten business casual pieces offer that, as well. Of course, "easy" is a relative term. Few things are easier than dropping your clothes off at the dry cleaner, which is what most Traditional Tailored and many Almost a Suit ensembles require.

When life allows you to dress down, your dry-cleaning bills shrink. Your washing machine, however, goes into overdrive, and so does your ironing board. What's more, a number of casual basics call for hand-washing with special care instructions.

It's up to you to make sure that your clothes are clean, pressed, and fresh. When you take good care of your business casual wardrobe, it returns the favor by rewarding you with years of fine service and good looks.

Here's how to care for your investment.

PANTS

CLEANING

✶ Pants made of wool, most wool blends, linen, and rayon gabardine must be professionally dry-cleaned. Dry-cleaning very frequently is not recommended for fine fabrics; in between cleanings, refresh your garments by brushing them (see below) or having them professionally pressed.

✶ Fine wool garments should be brushed after each wearing with a soft but firm-bristled brush. This will remove the dust that collects between the fibers of the fabric.

✶ Some trousers are made from washable wool, but check the label and be absolutely positive before attempting to launder them.

✶ Pants made of cotton, cotton-poly blends, or denim—including chinos, poplins, and twills—may be machine-washed and tumbled dry on a low setting. Use a warm iron if needed.

✶ Corduroy pants should be turned inside out before laundering.

PRESSING

✶ To spruce up creased trousers, you will need a press cloth (a cotton kitchen towel will do) and a spray water bottle. Spritz the area to be pressed, cover it with the cloth, and press—one leg at a time, please—using the appropriate fabric setting on your iron.

HANGING

✶ Remove the belt from the trousers and empty the pockets. Crease at the center front and center back and hang the pants from the bottom hem on a hanger that's specially made for trousers.

BLAZERS AND SPORT COATS

CLEANING

✶ Sport coats and blazers need to be professionally dry-cleaned no more than once or twice a year. Between wearings, brush your jackets—pockets emptied, buttons undone—with a soft-bristled yet fairly stiff brush. Use short, quick strokes, first upward and then down.

✶ If your blazer or sport coat becomes rumpled, hang it in the bathroom while you're taking a shower, and let it relax in the steam for ten minutes or so.

✶ You can also have your blazers and sport coats professionally pressed, which makes them look fresh but doesn't stress the fibers as too-frequent dry-cleaning does.

HANGING

✶ After each wearing, hang your jacket on a contoured hanger and let it rest, unbuttoned and pockets emptied, for at least twenty-four hours before wearing it again.

STORING

✶ Don't hang sport coats or blazers in plastic bags. Instead, use shoulder covers or cloth bags, which will protect the fabric from dust while still allowing it to breathe.

✶ If you live in moth country, you might consider having your high-quality wool blazers and sport coats put in cold storage off season. Many dry cleaners offer this service.

SHIRTS

CLEANING

✶ Shirts made of cotton can be machine-washed and -dried. Be sure to remove the shirt(s) from the dryer before they're 100 percent dry.

✶ Silk is highly absorbent, and so soiled silk shirts need to be washed promptly. Dry-cleaning or hand-washing is usually called for, but some silks are machine-washable. In any case, silks should be line-dried.

✶ Most rayon and linen shirts are either dry-clean-only or hand-wash items (although machine-washable linens are available).

✶ Hand-wash shirts in cool water with a mild soap, and drip-dry from a wooden or padded hanger.

PRESSING

✶ Keep cotton shirts damp until ready to press by spritzing them thoroughly with water and rolling them tightly in a bath towel. Use a warm to hot iron for 100 percent cottons, and a slightly lower setting for cotton blends. Don't press over the buttons, as this tends to cause breakage.

✶ Silk and rayon are sensitive to heat; press them on cooler settings.

✶ Linen should not be pressed bone-dry. Moisten the fabric with a spritz of water before pressing, then press it on a high setting.

SWEATERS

CLEANING

✶ For the most part, sweaters should either be hand-washed or professionally dry-cleaned, depending on the manufacturer's recommendation.

✶ Many cotton sweaters are machine-washable. For best results, turn the sweater inside out, wash using the delicate cycle, then tumble dry on a low setting.

HAND-WASHING

✳ Use tepid water and a mild soap that's recommended for woolens.

✳ Turn the sweater inside out and work the soapy water gently through the sweater, without twisting or stretching.

✳ Rinse the sweater in cold tap water.

✳ Repeat the process.

✳ Gently squeeze out excess water, then lay the sweater across a large terry-cloth towel.

✳ Roll the sweater in the towel and pat it.

✳ Place the sweater faceup on a dry towel and "block" it; that is, reshape it by hand into its original proportions.

MAINTENANCE

✳ Between wearings, shake out your sweater and let it air out by laying it flat on a cotton towel, away from direct sunlight.

✳ If your sweater develops "pills," gently razor them off. Don't attempt to pull at them, as this will damage the weave.

✳ If your sweater develops wrinkles or creases, hold a steam iron over—not on—the affected areas.

STORAGE

✳ Never hang a sweater. Instead, lay it flat in a cool, dry place.

✳ Sweaters should not be wrapped in plastic, as this will trap moisture. Natural, breathable storage boxes are a better bet.

✳ In the off-season, wool sweaters should be stored with mothballs or cedar chips.

BELTS

✳ Fabric belts can be spruced up using a good spot cleaner.

✳ Leather belts can be rid of minor nicks and scratches with shoe polish, but be sure to buff them well before wearing to avoid "ring around the waistband."

✳ Blemishes on suede or nubuck can be buffed out with a soft cloth.

TIES

CLEANING

✳ In years past, dry cleaners used to take ties apart, clean them, then stitch them back together. Today's modern dry-cleaning methods may tend to flatten the hand-rolled edges of fine ties. Therefore, consider spot-cleaning as an option.

✳ To remove a spot from a silk tie, first steam it (i.e., hang it over the curtain rod while you're taking a shower). Then dip the skinny end of the tie in a good spot remover solution. Use the skinny end to briskly rub the spot, moving in the direction of the weave.

✳ When all else fails, save your spotty silk ties and wear them under sweaters or sweater vests.

✳ Knit ties may be hand-washed in cool water using mild detergent. Dry them flat on a towel.

STORING

✻ Always store your ties untied, and resist the temptation of simply loosening your tie and pulling it over your head, which can create a permanent dimple in the silk.

✻ Don't hang knit ties (cotton knits tend to stretch). Rather, roll them up.

SHOES

CLEANING

✻ Fabric shoes can be spot-cleaned using a mild detergent and a soft brush. Rinse with warm water, pat with a towel, then air-dry.

✻ Leather shoes may be brushed with a horsehair brush and cleaned with saddle soap, which also conditions and preserves leather. Do not use saddle soap on oil-tanned leather.

✻ Suede shoes are usually cleaned by brushing, using short, quick strokes. Some spots can be removed using an art gum eraser; if the suede is scarred, however, try gently removing the mark with fine sandpaper.

POLISHING

✻ Before polishing leather shoes, clean them with saddle soap.

✻ Apply a small amount of cream polish to a soft cloth.

✻ Using circular motions, rub the cream into the leather, beginning at the toes.

✻ Fold up the cloth and buff each shoe.

✻ Shine with a clean, soft cloth.

STORAGE AND MAINTENANCE

✻ Use a shoehorn when you put on a shoe.

✻ Store shoes on wooden shoe trees to help maintain their shape (shoes won't "breathe" on plastic).

✻ If your suede shoes get wet, stuff them with newspaper until they're thoroughly dry.

✻ Rotate your shoe wardrobe. Wearing the same pair day in and day out doesn't give the leather a chance to breathe properly.

✻ When traveling, pack your shoes in shoe bags to prevent scratching and rubbing on your clothing.

IN CONCLUSION

The world keeps turning. These days, an interest in one's appearance and a penchant for clothes-shopping isn't divided along gender lines—at least among people under thirty. Boys who grew up with the *Free to Be . . . You and Me* sensibilities of the 1970s are men now, and they're taking control of their own look. Working out is just the beginning; they also dye their hair, tan year-round, schedule routine facials, whiten their teeth, get wax jobs, and shop intensely for clothes that look great and express their individuality.

Bottom line: You've got competition in the personal presentation department. And chances are it will only get tougher with time.

Yes, it's a shame that our society is so shallow that belts and blazers matter. In a perfect world, we'd all be judged on the basis of our talent, intelligence, and good ideas. It does happen—fashion disaster Bill Gates is doing okay, right?—but unless you're a bona fide genius riding a rocket to the top of the Fortune 500, it's best to do yourself a favor and dress smart.

Whether you're balancing books, managing a department, running a company, or running errands, the right outfits will help smooth the path you're on. Doors won't automatically open just because you've matched a crisp shirt with well-tailored trousers, but they won't automatically close, either.

Someday, what you wear won't matter. Your accomplishments will be the only wardrobe you'll need. Until you become king of the hill, however, there are only a few things that you have complete control over. Clothes is one of them.

So, what are you waiting for? Seize your style. Conquer your closet. Make fashion a slave to you. Go forth and prosper, and may you never have an uncomfortable moment.

INDEX

ABOUT LANDS' END

LANDS' END is a direct merchant of classically inspired clothing and home products offered through specialty catalogs, on the Internet, and in Sears stores. Celebrating its fortieth anniversary in 2003, Lands' End is world renowned for its customer service and "Guaranteed. Period.®" approach to customer satisfaction. For more information about Lands' End, visit www.landsend.com.

ABOUT THE AUTHOR

TODD LYON is an artist-turned-writer who has authored or coauthored more than a dozen books focused on fashion, food, business, and fun, including *Chic Simple: Cooking, The Domain Book of Intuitive Home Design, The New Year's Eve Compendium, The Intuitive Businesswoman,* and *How to Buy Your Perfect Wedding Dress.* Her articles and essays have appeared in the *New York Times* and the *Boston Globe,* as well as in *Cosmopolitan, Biography, Saveur,* and *Bust* magazines; currently, she is a columnist for the *New Haven Register,* her hometown paper.